CHRIS RISER

BLESSED

Beatitudes for Kingdom Living

Blessed
Beatitudes for Kingdom Living
By Chris Riser

Copyright ©2022 by Chris Riser.
All rights reserved.

No part of this book may be reproduced by any means without written consent of the publisher except for brief quotes used in reviews written specifically for use in a magazine or newspaper.

Scripture taken from the New American Standard Bible,
©1960, 1962, 1963, 1971, 1972, 1973, 1975, 1977, 1995
by The Lockman Foundation.
Used by permission.

Cover design by Jessica Mohr

ISBN 979-8-9867186-0-6

Printed in the United States of America
by 48 Hour Books.

Published by

Maryville, TN
www.gracemaryville.org

BLESSED

Beatitudes for Kingdom Living

To Alisa — no words can truly express how thankful I am for your partnership in the pursuit of kingdom living.

Acknowledgments

This book would have been impossible apart from the faithful labor of others who share a passion for living and communicating the truth of God's Word. Thank you to those who did the hard work of slogging through the early editions of the book and providing essential feedback: Mary Cozzolino, Yvonne Hanson, Amy Lundell, and Ronald Martin. My deep appreciation to Patty Brown for graciously and excellently doing all the formatting. A special thank you to Jessica Mohr for spending countless hours listening to the sermons upon which this book is based, converting them into manuscript form, and tracking down all the quotations and references (along with providing suggestions for additional illustrations and a host of other essential feedback). This book exists because Jessica willed it to be so! Perhaps my greatest thanks goes to the faithful congregation of Grace Community Church in Maryville, Tennessee who, for these past eighteen years, have gladly humbled their hearts under the preaching of Word of God and have been used of the Lord to build a little "preview of the Kingdom" here in the foothills of the Smokies.

Table of Contents

Introduction

J esus is the King! From beginning to end, the gospel of Matthew testifies to the reality that Jesus Christ is the Lord and Master of the universe, the Ruler of His chosen people Israel, the Sovereign over the hearts of men, and the one true King who will reign forevermore. Matthew not only aimed to present a clear and compelling picture of Jesus as Lord, but to call every reader to receive the rich benefits of His rule by entering into His kingdom.

The kingdom of God, however, cannot be entered through normal human means. Royal birth or perfect pedigree do not guarantee entry. The kingdom is neither taken by force nor infiltrated by subterfuge. No amount of money is sufficient to purchase admittance. No level of human achievement or greatness can earn citizenship. The King must personally grant His approval to any would-be citizen. Yet Matthew powerfully demonstrates that *no one* is worthy of such favor. The tension within the book of Matthew, then, is that while citizenship in God's kingdom is supremely desirable, no earthly means of gaining access exist.

Enter the Beatitudes. The vast majority of Americans have heard the phrase "Blessed are . . .", yet unsurprisingly mainstream culture misconstrues the word's meaning. Too often it has been reduced to the clichéd hashtag on social media (#blessed) that has served many as a subtle way to "humble-brag" about accomplishments.[1] Even within Christian circles the term is vaguely generic at best and dangerously misused at worst.

More specifically, the Beatitudes have been co-opted throughout the centuries by a wide variety of movements, each with its own agenda. They've been widely interpreted as an external system of moralism; still others have tied them to radical political ideologies translated through the lens of socioeconomic oppression.

My aim with this book is to demonstrate that Matthew's presentation of the Beatitudes is informed by the purpose of his gospel. Jesus' statements concerning those who are blessed function as instructions on how to enter His kingdom and receive its full benefits. These promises are not merely (or even primarily) solace for society's materially marginalized, or a kind of "chicken soup" for the Christian soul, but are the means of exposing everyone as naked and needy before a holy God. The Beatitudes form the gateway through which the larger message of the Sermon on the Mount is revealed: *The true standard of righteous living required in the kingdom of heaven is only reached by those who have been born again through the living and abiding Word of God.*

To that end there are several considerations which will prove helpful to the reader as you prepare to have your heart exposed by our Savior's piercing words. First is the matter of identity. The Beatitudes force us to consider who we really are and who we desire to be. The world seeks to shape us according to its mold so that we view ourselves in light of various cultural constructs: "I am an American

---

1. Jessica Bennett, "They Feel 'Blessed,'" *New York Times*, May 2, 2014, https://www.nytimes.com.

citizen," "I am a wife and mother," "I am an engineer," "I am a social justice warrior," and so on.

Yet the primary focus of Matthew's gospel, as reflected in the Beatitudes, is that the most important aspect of our identity is how we are related to the kingdom of God. Jesus' words relentlessly press us to view ourselves through God's perspective and to desire to be most fundamentally known as heavenly citizens—God's children. All other identities are subsumed in Christ as we seek first His kingdom by pursuing the attributes of blessedness found in Jesus' words.

Next, we must carefully evaluate our goals and pursuits—those things which we believe will make us truly happy. We are persistently told that our satisfaction will be found in achieving some temporal dream (the right family size, a satisfying career, Instagram "influencer" status, TikTok virality, etc.).

Yet the real message of blessedness is that our satisfaction can only be found in Christ, and the pursuit of being conformed to His image. The believer is never assured of any earthly pleasure, but Christ's words in this passage guarantee full satisfaction to those who hunger and thirst for righteousness. Indeed, the greatest pleasure in the universe is to "see God"—to obtain a true, intimate relationship with the eternal Creator of the universe—and it is this very sight which is promised as a result of genuine blessedness.

We must also judiciously assess our expectations of the lives we are granted here on earth. Too often peddlers of a prosperity gospel promise the kingdom of heaven on earth—or at least their version of it: optimal health, enjoyable toys, relative security and comfort, and a nice ride. But the message of the Beatitudes shatters this treacherous facade. Jesus' stunning claim is that the blessed mourn and the persecuted rejoice, not in their veritable cornucopia of earthly trinkets, but in the privilege of suffering like Jesus and the prophets before Him.

There is certainly great earthly benefit which comes from being blessed of God, but it does not take the form of worldly fulfillments. Mercy, joy, holiness, and spiritual comfort are all promised to the blessed one, but these gifts come in the midst of trial and persecution, not comfort and ease. Instead of the world's praise, Jesus guarantees insult. In the place of recognition, slander. The outlook of the blessed one is not temporal, but eternal. Our King calls us to "rejoice and be glad, for [our] reward in heaven is great" (Matt. 5:12).

Next, there is the issue of means. How does one become "blessed"? The dangers here are myriad. Some may pursue the blessings of Christ's sermon through human effort and external habit—redoubling their efforts and making new resolutions every time they fail. Others might take the more "spiritual" approach: "waiting" for the Spirit of God, "letting go" of their grip on the "wheel of life," or perhaps listening for a "still, small voice" to nudge them in a particular direction of blessing.

Yet Scripture reveals the only path to blessedness comes first through the hearing of God's Word, followed by the supernatural work of the Holy Spirit to transform the heart—resulting in repentance and faith—and continued through Spirit-empowered effort by means of prayer, the Word, and the church. Even our truly Christ-motivated efforts, however, never earn or cause blessedness, but are ever and always the result of God's gracious work through His indwelling Spirit. This is humbling to us. We are always looking for something that will promote our statuses and stroke our egos. But the one who would be blessed must be "poor in spirit," recognizing his total inadequacy and dependency upon the Lord Jesus who alone brings true blessing.

Finally, this book must be read in light of community. The pursuit of blessedness is never purely individual. This work is not intended as a manifesto on how an individual believer can bring down the blessings of God upon himself—even with a humble, contrite spirit. When Jesus says blessed are "you," He is using the second person plural, referring to the community of the saints, the people of God.

Blessedness comes to those who mourn, who are gentle, humble, merciful, pure in heart, and peacemakers—*within the body of*

Christ. Matthew is clear that Christ came to build His church, and it is through this body that true blessedness flows. *If we cut ourselves off from the community of God's people, then we will not experience God's blessing, nor will the rest of the church be blessed.* Our Lord desires the work of blessedness to begin in the heart of the individual believer, but always to extend outward to His people corporately, and then throughout the entire world.

These are heavy challenges with which to begin a book simply titled *Blessed,* but it is my prayer that every reader will experience the true blessing that comes from being a part of the kingdom of heaven. Where hearts are tired and weary, I pray that Christ's words will provide comfort and strength. For those who are in a season of joy and encouragement, my hope is that these truths will bring greater growth and maturity.

Perhaps it may even be that entrance to the kingdom comes in the midst of reading with a first-time recognition of the true nature of God's blessing. In every way, for every season, may this blessing of Christ be extended to each reader — to the praise and honor of His glorious name.

~ The Beatitudes ~

¹*When Jesus saw the crowds, He went up on the mountain; and after He sat down, His disciples came to Him.*

²*He opened His mouth and began to teach them, saying,*

³*"Blessed are the poor in spirit, for theirs is the kingdom of heaven.*

⁴*"Blessed are those who mourn, for they shall be comforted.*

⁵*"Blessed are the gentle, for they shall inherit the earth.*

⁶*"Blessed are those who hunger and thirst for righteousness, for they shall be satisfied.*

⁷*"Blessed are the merciful, for they shall receive mercy.*

⁸*"Blessed are the pure in heart, for they shall see God.*

⁹*"Blessed are the peacemakers, for they shall be called sons of God.*

¹⁰*"Blessed are those who have been persecuted for the sake of righteousness, for theirs is the kingdom of heaven.*

¹¹*"Blessed are you when people insult you and persecute you, and falsely say all kinds of evil against you because of Me.* ¹²*Rejoice and be glad, for your reward in heaven is great; for in the same way they persecuted the prophets who were before you."*

Chapter 1

Blessedness

When Jesus saw the crowds, He went up on the mountain;
and after He sat down, His disciples came to Him. He
opened His mouth and began to teach them, saying...

Due in large part to social media, "blessed" has been a term bandied about with increasing frequency in recent years. From posting picturesque vacation shots and ripped gym selfies to sports accomplishments and food pics, the world publicly declares itself happy. Its profession of grateful contentment, however, does not appear to comport with reality. Suicide is rapidly becoming a leading cause of death.[1] Combined with drug overdose, both now account for the reduction in U.S. life expectancy.[2] Reports of depression

---

1. "Leading Causes of Death," Centers for Disease Control & Prevention, accessed January 12, 2022, https://www.cdc.gov/nchs/fastats/leading-causes-of-death.htm.
2. Michael Devitt, "CDC Data Show U.S. Life Expectancy Continues to Decline," American Academy of Family Physicians, December 10, 2018, https://www.aafp.org/news/health-of-the-public/20181210lifeexpectdrop.html.

have quadrupled among American adults since the recent global pandemic.[3] Eating disorders in young women are positively correlated to time spent on Instagram.[4] These statistics don't appear to square with the untold millions who are dutifully following their hearts' desires — or perhaps they do. Who is truly blessed? What does that mean? Does the world know? Do evangelicals even know, or do they too find the concept somewhat elusive, even wrongly invoking it?

While God blesses in many ways, the pronounced blessings of Christ's Beatitudes are quite specific. We tend to limit blessings to favorable external circumstances, certainly not internal heart attitudes rooted in a lowly self-estimation. Yet our Savior's Beatitudes are just that, "diametrical opposites to what the world holds up" as blessed. Instead of "self-importance, self-fulfillment, [and] self-satisfaction," Jesus grounded them in self-denial.[5] Knowing they've been misinterpreted throughout the centuries, the Beatitudes must be carefully studied to understand them properly. They mark the beginning of Christ's most prolific sermon ever recorded. Through the Sermon on the Mount, the book of Matthew reveals that Christ's righteousness is absolutely necessary to not only gain entrance into His kingdom, but to faithfully live within it. Stretching across three chapters (Matt. 5–7), the sermon's underlying theme is encapsulated in this introductory benediction referred to as the Beatitudes. Both they and the entire sermon reveal the true standard of righteous living required in the kingdom. This standard, we will discover, is only possible for those who have been born again to the living and abiding Word of God.

3. Jillian McKoy, "Depression Rates in US Tripled When Pandemic First Hit — Now They're Even Worse," *The Brink*, Boston University, October 7, 2021, https://www. bu.edu/articles/2021/depression-rates-tripled-when-pandemic-first-hit.
4. Kim Elsesser, "Here's How Instagram Harms Young Women According to Research," *Forbes*, October 5, 2021, https://www.forbes.com.
5. Ligon Duncan, "Matthew: The Citizens of the Kingdom I" (sermon), First Presbyterian Church, Jackson, MS, April 1, 1997, https://fpcjackson.org.

The Background of the Beatitudes

Time & Place

Christ began His earthly ministry on the heels of His baptism and the forty days of temptation in the wilderness. John the Baptist had been taken into custody, completing the forerunner's mission. Traveling from town to town, Christ was an itinerant preacher in the region of Galilee, proclaiming the nature of the kingdom over which He presided and healing many from physical afflictions. Matthew's account of Christ's ministry was not necessarily recorded chronologically, but it still seems that the sermon was delivered fairly early. It most likely occurred at some point after the twelve disciples were chosen. Word had spread of His healing miracles, so large crowds were beginning to follow Him. He had compassion on both their material and spiritual needs. As a pattern of His ministry, Christ physically healed but also took time to teach the truths of "the gospel of the kingdom" (Matt. 4:23). Though many were blind to their desperate spiritual conditions, Christ offered the infinitely more important cure to the disease of their souls.

It was delivered most likely on the northern edge of the Sea of Galilee. While Matthew described the setting as going up a "mountain," American minds would perceive the topography surrounding the northern coastline as more akin to verdant, rolling hills. The gently sloping hillside would have offered accessibility and served as a natural stage. His voice and appearance would be much more perceptible to the hordes of gatherers. Christ found this suitable for His purposes, even at times reversing the positioning by standing on the shoreline or in a boat as if in an amphitheater. Either way it was important to Him that those coming hear His preaching.

Speaker

Counterintuitive to our cultural sensibilities, Christ did not stand up as any speaker in our day. Matthew purposely mentioned that He sat down before preaching which had serious significance in their society.

While a seated speaker to us might convey an air of informality, it meant the opposite to the Jewish people in Christ's time. The seated position expressed authority. When a rabbi sat down with his followers surrounding him, it served as a behavioral indicator that he was about to formally teach—what he said from that point on was to be taken as official, authoritative instruction. The posture was a very clear method of communication to distinguish from regular conversation. At the conclusion of Jesus' sermon, Matthew recorded that the crowds were "amazed at His teaching; for He was teaching them as one having authority" (7:28). Of course, His authority extends infinitely beyond any earthly teacher. The King of kings and Lord of lords was making a divine pronouncement about His kingdom and its citizens. The truths contained therein are as much applicable to us today as they were then. It is therefore incumbent upon us to carefully understand and properly appraise every beatitude in our Savior's sermon.

Audience

The text informs us that Christ's disciples came to Him after He assumed the position to teach. It seems that Matthew desired to draw a distinction between His disciples and the host of others who were following them. Among His disciples are not only the chosen twelve but others who professed and believed Jesus to be the long-awaited Messiah. Time would reveal the validity of each confession, but many no doubt had saving faith and were true followers. They would embrace Christ's call to deny themselves, take up their crosses, and follow after Him (Luke 9:23). The thrust of the sermon aimed at life in the kingdom and was thus directed at those already in it. While the unbelieving listeners would deem these standards for righteousness a shocking impossibility, Christ expected this manner of living from true kingdom citizens who would be given the Holy Spirit. Aware of the crowds hearing His words as well, He knew these truths would drive them to either accept or reject Him as their Messiah.

The Context of the Beatitudes

As noted, the characteristics that comprised life in the kingdom were the central theme of both the Beatitudes and the sermon as a whole. Since the inception of His ministry Christ had been proclaiming, "Repent, for the kingdom of heaven is at hand" (Matt. 4:17). Repentance and faith gained admission into the kingdom, but He also described the nature of kingdom life itself. The sermon as a whole outlined the blessed state of this kingdom, the character of its citizens, the righteousness that defines it, and who's inside and outside of it.

Other Interpretations

Through the centuries, many have distorted the sermon's meaning for another more suited to their own various ends. Unbelievers have professed appreciation for the morality it contains, for example, though they fundamentally misunderstand it. Well-known humanitarian and activist Mahatma Gandhi embraced this particular sermon and incorporated his understanding of it into his own false belief system.

Contemporary culture, like Gandhi, tends to view the discourse as a treatise on ethical behavior for the moral improvement of humanity in general. The world views Christ as a great teacher and reformer who desired for men to live in peace and love. However, Gandhi and everyone else share a common problem—they can't live up to the standards Christ set forth which He summed up in one excerpt: "Therefore you are to be perfect, as your heavenly Father is perfect" (5:48).

Serving as the introduction to the sermon, the Beatitudes haven't escaped this treatment unscathed. Alexander Maclaren stoutly observed over a century ago:

> People talk a great deal, and a good deal of it very
> insincerely, about their admiration for these precepts
> gathered together in this chapter (Matt. 5). If they
> would try to live them for a fortnight, they would

perhaps pause a little longer than some of them do before they said, as do people that detest the theology of the New Testament, "The Sermon on the Mount is my religion." Is it? It does not look very like it.[6] (parentheses added)

In his commentary, R.T. France points out, "Jesus' typical use of extreme, black-and-white categories lays down a challenge which cannot be simply converted into a set of rules and regulations for life in the real world."[7] Outside of Christ's work and the Spirit's power, this holiness is impossible. Yet the world gets this understanding wrong, regarding the Beatitudes as aimed instead at society's downtrodden in life. Others have appropriated and repurposed them to fit radical socioeconomic ideologies rooted in ideas of systemic oppression. Both liberation theology and progressive Christianity erroneously celebrate the entire sermon as politically "subversive," "countercultural," to and a "call to resistance."[8]

Even among sound theological circles, some believe the sermon is describing the forthcoming millennial kingdom, but this interpretation creates a host of problems:

> First of all, the text does not indicate or imply that these teachings are for another age. Second, Jesus demanded them of people who were not living in the Millennium. Third, many of the teachings themselves become meaningless if they are applied to the Millennium. Just look through the sermon. It talks about being persecuted for your faith. That doesn't happen in the Millennium. . . . Fourth, every princi-

6. Alexander Maclaren, *The Gospel According to St. Matthew* (New York: A. C. Armstrong & Son, 1905), 147–148.

7. R. T. France, *The Gospel of Matthew*, ed. Gordon Fee, *The New International Commentary on the New Testament* (Grand Rapids: Eerdmans, 2007), 154.

8. Lindsey Paris-Lopez, "The Sermon on the Mount: A Theology of Resistance," *Sojourners*, February 10, 2017, https://sojo.net/articles/sermon-mount-theology-resistance.

ple taught in the Sermon on the Mount is also taught elsewhere in the New Testament in contexts that clearly apply to believers of our present age. Fifth, there are many New Testament passages that command equally impossible standards, which unglorified human strength cannot continually achieve.[9]

Some believe the sermon is exclusively evangelistic in purpose. While the sermon can certainly have that effect by driving to the cross those who realize they fall woefully short of the righteousness laid out, it does not appear to be the *primary* intention of Christ's sermon. Indeed, some scholars believe He heightened the law's demands to chiefly highlight the impossibility of obedience: "You've heard this, but I say this." This was not an exaggerated emphasis or re-interpretation; He was simply shedding light on the godly heart attitudes that had always been inherent within the law. While true obedience from the heart was impossible for unbelievers, it wasn't for Christians indwelt by the Holy Spirit.

Purpose

Instead, Christ's principal focus, as previously stated, was on the nature of kingdom life itself. He chiefly addressed His true followers by giving a presentation of Spirit-filled living in anticipation of both His and the Holy Spirit's forthcoming work on the cross and in the heart, respectively. This allowed the sermon to function secondarily as a means to point men to salvation by grace through faith in Christ, but first and foremost as instruction for believers in the church age under the New Covenant:

> Far from being a philosophical discourse on ethics, this is a messianic manifesto, setting out the

---

9. John MacArthur, *Matthew 1–7*, vol. 1, *The MacArthur New Testament Commentary* (Chicago: Moody Press, 1985), 138.

unique demands and revolutionary insights of one who claims absolute authority over other people and whose word, like the word of God, will determine their destiny. No wonder the crowds were astonished, not only by the teaching but even more by the teacher.[10]

The underlying linchpin in both of these purposes is the necessity of rebirth. As Christ told Nicodemus, "Unless one is born again he cannot see the kingdom of God" (John 3:3). The sermon as a whole, and the Beatitudes in particular, are predicated on this reality. Only those whose hearts have been changed can exemplify the character of those who are blessed, but these internal heart attitudes are necessary for initial entrance into the kingdom. God's work of regeneration must occur since man's natural heart is fundamentally incapable of reflecting God's holy character.

For example, the very first beatitude commends an internal poorness of spirit. This humility of heart wrought by God is required to enter into the kingdom through salvation, but Jesus taught the inner attitude must continue and increase in order to flourish within His realm as a faithful citizen. In declaring this, He carried all the authority of a King who decides the inner workings of His kingdom. Christ's specifications assume a perfect standard. The standard never changes, although we do. Positionally, we are clothed with His perfection at salvation, but we thrive in the kingdom as we are conformed to His image through sanctification. This process of pursuing godliness should be our highest goal. It's where our blessings lie. Christ expects the church to live out the standards He outlined in this sermon by the empowerment of the indwelling Spirit.

This character for righteous living is addressed in the Beatitudes and much of the sermon as a whole. The Father is glorified when we

---

10. France, *Matthew* (2007), 156.

look like His Son, and the Son's highest desire is to see His Father glorified. God uses our righteous living to draw others to Himself: "Let your light shine before men in such a way that they may see your good works, and glorify your Father who is in heaven" (Matt. 5:16).

Godliness is also radical. Christ revealed in the sermon that we are guilty before God based on the state of our hearts alone so that anger toward a brother in the heart, for instance, warrants the same sentence of fiery hell that a murder conviction receives (vv. 21–22). Sin is so serious Christ advocated extreme measures to avoid it, from metaphorically chopping off hands to plucking out eyes (vv. 29–30).

Not only extreme, holy living is also grounded in love. All of God's commands are bound up in love which in turn drives their obedience. We can successfully love our neighbor as we obey His precepts. Only believers can truly fulfill the law of love even toward enemies: "You have heard that it was said, 'YOU SHALL LOVE YOUR NEIGHBOR and hate your enemy.' But I say to you, love your enemies and pray for those who persecute you, so that you may be sons of your Father who is in heaven" (vv. 43–45). This caliber of love enables us to live righteously in the midst of the greatest persecution from the darkest of enemies.

In stark contrast, *self*-righteous living leads to hell by way of legalism. Although they look similar on the outside, God sees the heart. Christ warned, "Beware of practicing your righteousness before men to be noticed by them; otherwise, you have no reward with your Father who is in heaven" (6:1). External self-righteousness is not only devoid of any real holiness, but it also condemns its practicer to eternal condemnation. Even believers who mimic this sinful behavior not done for God's glory will find the efforts worthless, wasted, and without reward. Ultimately, though, the unbeliever's heart will be exposed:

> Not everyone who says to Me, "Lord, Lord," will enter the kingdom of heaven, but he who does the

will of My Father who is in heaven will enter. Many will say to Me on that day, "Lord, Lord, did we not prophesy in Your name, and in Your name cast out demons, and in Your name perform many miracles?" And then I will declare to them, "I never knew you; DEPART FROM ME, YOU WHO PRACTICE LAWLESSNESS." (7:21–23)

True godliness should reflect a converted heart since "every good tree bears good fruit" (7:17); it exercises an eternal perspective and doesn't store up "treasures on earth, where moth and rust destroy, and where thieves break in and steal" (6:19). Christ commanded, "But seek first [God's] kingdom and His righteousness" (6:33). Christ concluded the sermon by affirming that His true disciples would hear His words and act on them (7:24), so it behooves us to remember this as we explore the introductory jewels of His masterful sermon. *Plumbing the depths of the Beatitudes is not exclusively an intellectual exercise, but a deep, heartfelt self-examination of the inner man.* Paul exhorted the Corinthians: "Test yourselves to see if you are in the faith; examine yourselves! Or do you not recognize this about yourselves, that Jesus Christ is in you—unless indeed you fail the test?" (2 Cor. 13:5)

If you, dear reader, find no resemblance between the character sketched in the Beatitudes and your own, crying out to God in repentance and faith may be in order. But even for believers, we must recommit ourselves to strive for the radical obedience to which our King is calling us. As kingdom citizens we must increasingly bear His image through hearts that flow out in lives that redound to His glory.

The Meaning of "Beatitude"

While the term *beatitude* is defined as a general state of blessedness, it has also come to exclusively reference the blessings Christ pronounced in the Sermon on the Mount.[11] So what is *blessedness*? What does it mean to be *blessed*? As mentioned, mainstream culture has appropriated the word. Even the worldliest may use it in casual conversation as a manner of speaking. Many exclusively associate it with material manifestation in health, finances, and worldly success. In reality, blessedness has nothing to do with the temporal health and wholeness men crave. *True blessedness pertains to being rightly related to the King.* Matthew employs the Greek term *makarios* which can translate as "blessed" or "happy":

> It implies a congratulatory element as recognizing the desirability of the condition felicitated. In the New Testament it is always a strongly religious concept denoting an inner quality of life, a joy and happiness not dependent upon favorable external circumstances. . . . It points to a state of soul that the believer begins to experience in his life, even amid adverse outward circumstances, but its full bliss will be realized only in the future life.[12]

The nature of true blessedness is bound up in God's favor. Even though this should be humanity's primary concern, men seek the favor of those around them instead—their bosses and peers, the culture, and themselves. Society's notion of blessedness finds happiness in everything other than God, the true source of ultimate satisfaction.

Christ's Beatitudes turn the world's idea of blessedness on its head, but it's not a radical change of one's political, socioeconomic, or even physical condition. It's a change of heart. *To be a part of the kingdom is to be blessed, and to be truly blessed is to live within it in a manner that's contrary to the natural man's ideas.* Studying the Beatitudes

11. *Merriam-Webster.com Dictionary*, s.v. "beatitude," accessed November 11, 2021, https://www.merriam-webster.com/dictionary/beatitude.
12. D. Edmond Hiebert, *James* (Chicago: Moody Press, 1992), 82–83.

in-depth, we will see how blessedness actually means to possess humility rather than pride; to mourn rather than laugh; to gently yield rather than brazenly assert; to hunger for holiness instead of pleasure; to give mercy instead of what's deserved; to possess purity of heart rather than self-righteous works; to make peace instead of insisting on our own way; and to endure the persecution and insults of the world rather than enjoy its acceptance and praise. That is the blessed nature of the kingdom that the outside world cannot accurately appraise.

As a Western-state transplant to the South, I've often overheard the well-worn phrase "bless his heart." Its construction implies a blessing from God is needed due to the flawed character of the person mentioned. In Jesus' sermon, however, His blessings are preceded by the godly characteristics that warrant such blessings. We may define blessedness as *joyful contentment which flows from being a recipient of God's loving, kind, and unmerited favor*. It's not a superficial happiness but a deep-seated satisfaction. Breaking it down, we first ought to recognize that blessedness is essentially rooted in God Himself. Scripture declares:

> Blessed be the LORD God, the God of Israel,
> Who alone works wonders.
> And blessed be His glorious name forever;
> And may the whole earth be filled with His glory.
> (Ps. 72:18–19)

It may seem confusing that the Bible blesses God because we already know His blessedness — not to mention He's the One whose name we invoke to dispense blessing! But blessing God is a way to express His worthiness. Scripture recognizes and affirms that God, by His character and nature, is fully and perfectly satisfied within Himself. Paul and Peter both declared, "Blessed be the God and Father of our Lord Jesus Christ" (Eph. 1:3; 1 Pet. 1:3). Many times, we breeze past these epistolary introductions and forget the meaning of what we're reading. They are professing that God alone is worthy of all praise, honor, and worship because of who He is. In fact, His blessing to us is our motivation to turn around and bless Him. Unlike God, we do not have the intrinsic foundation upon which to merit blessing, so if we are blessed by Him, it must flow through His own character and worthiness. We acknowledge that "every good thing given and every perfect gift is from above, coming down from the Father of lights" (James 1:17).

After understanding that all blessings of supreme joy emanate from God Himself, we find that our blessedness likewise comes from being "partakers of the divine nature" (2 Pet. 1:4). Only those who are clothed with Christ's righteousness can ever be truly blessed. Taken in context, Peter revealed:

> His divine power has granted to us everything pertaining to life and godliness, through the true knowledge of Him who called us by His own glory and excellence. For by these He has granted to us His precious and magnificent promises, so that by them you may become partakers of the divine nature, having escaped the corruption that is in the world by lust. (2 Pet. 1:3–4)

Those who share in God's very nature are those who are in the kingdom. God regenerates believers and grants them a new nature enabled to participate in His blessedness. The person and work of Christ provided this opportunity. He plucked us out of the "domain of darkness, and transferred us to the kingdom of His beloved Son, in whom we have redemption, the forgiveness of sins" (Col. 1:13–14). Through our union in Christ and the perfect righteousness imputed to our accounts, He lavishly pours out blessings upon us, granting us everything we truly need. By His own glorious, excellent character He imparted the precious new nature that gains us entrance into His magnificent kingdom. He has done away with our former corrupt nature that tainted our mind, will, and desires. He brought the truth of

His Word to bear in bringing our dead hearts to new life and placed His own nature within us through the indwelling Holy Spirit. The Spirit, in turn, cleanses and reorients us so that we think properly and desire Him as we should: "There is no blessedness, no perfect contentedness and joy of the sort of which Jesus speaks here, except that which comes from a personal relationship to Him."[13]

The essence of this biblical joy transcends circumstance. Sadly, many of us determine happiness by the net result of the day's events according to our own evaluation. This can even happen in ministry. Our church participates in door-to-door evangelism, and while some teams may return after much interaction with residents, others may return without a single conversation or opportunity to share the gospel. Typically, the teams will understandably have different emotional responses, but we must realize that God is good in both situations. His goodness and blessing to us are not dependent upon how many doors open. What matters is that we belong to Him. The seventy disciples who were sent out by Christ returned to Him "with joy, saying, 'Lord, even the demons are subject to us in Your name'" (Luke 10:17). Christ welcomed their return, but warned, "Nevertheless do not rejoice in this, that the spirits are subject to you, but rejoice that your names are recorded in heaven" (v. 20). We rejoice over our kingdom citizenship from which our ultimate blessing of salvation comes.

Our highest blessing lies in having our sins forgiven. Paul cited King David when arguing for justification by faith alone:

> But to the one who does not work, but believes in Him who justifies the ungodly, his faith is credited as righteousness, just as David also speaks of the blessing on the man to whom God credits righteousness apart from works:

---

13. MacArthur, *Matthew* (1985), 142.

"BLESSED ARE THOSE WHOSE LAWLESS DEEDS HAVE

BEEN FORGIVEN,

AND WHOSE SINS HAVE BEEN COVERED.

"BLESSED IS THE MAN WHOSE SIN THE LORD WILL

NOT TAKE INTO ACCOUNT." (Rom. 4:5–8)

John MacArthur explains,

> To be blessed is not a superficial feeling of well-being based on circumstance, but a deep supernatural experience of contentedness based on the fact that one's life is right with God. . . . Blessedness is based on objective reality, realized in the miracle of transformation to a new and divine nature.[14]

This should be the foundation upon which we approach each day and appraise every circumstance. Otherwise, our emotions will rise and fall, ebb and flow, and we will feel both blessed and cursed.

The beatific promises Christ preached for kingdom citizens are not merely a byproduct of His saving work—He fully desires us to experience blessing. He purposely designed us to find satisfaction in Him alone. Far from the cosmic killjoy unbelievers accuse Him of being, God desires to save men from their tragic state unto a matchless bliss that only He can provide.

In the sermon Jesus carefully and clearly laid out the way of blessedness. In fact, far from the temporal, limited, and volatile happiness the world chases after on earth, the eternal, unfathomable, and immutable kingdom Jesus described is the true "good life." As we press into the Beatitudes in the coming chapters, may our character be increasingly conformed to the image of Christ so that His blessedness might flow out of us in the refreshing stream of a holy, God-glorifying lifestyle.

---

14. MacArthur, *Matthew* (1985), 142.

Questions for Reflection & Discussion

1. When and where did Jesus deliver the Sermon on the Mount? What was the significance of him sitting to teach? Who comprised His audience?

2. Read through the entire sermon (Matt. 5–7) and record three main thoughts here.

3. Describe one alternative interpretation of the Beatitudes and/or the Sermon on the Mount as a whole. Why is this problematic?

4. What is the primary purpose of the Sermon on the Mount in general and the Beatitudes in particular (meant for believers)? What is the secondary purpose (meant for unbelievers)? What is the "underlying linchpin" both of these purposes are predicated on (see John 3:3)?

5. What's the difference between entering Christ's kingdom and living within it? This will be mentioned all throughout this book. (Hint: *Think justification and sanctification*.)

6. Righteous living and self-righteous living have two very different end results. What is the result of the latter (see Matt. 7:21–23)? What does 2 Corinthians 13:5 command us to do?

7. Define *blessedness*. Where does it come from? Why do we bless God? What does that mean? How are we able to receive blessing?

8. What is the highest blessing a person can receive? With this in mind, what can the believer *always* rejoice in, even when enduring the most painful trials in life?

9. Pray for God to use your study of the Beatitudes to further conform your heart to Christ's image.

Chapter 2

Blessed Are the Poor in Spirit

Blessed are the poor in spirit,
for theirs is the kingdom of heaven.

Residents of Wasatch County, Utah, were in for a surprise in 2019 when they learned a 1,500 sq. ft. home was overvalued by almost $1 billion. The home, built on two acres in 1978, should have been valued around $300,000, but a staff member in the assessor's office believed the error was inputted into the system when he accidentally dropped a phone on his keyboard. The mishap resulted in "a countywide overvaluation of more than $6 million and revenue shortfalls."[1] Much to their dismay, county officials warned taxpayers of higher rates over the next several years to offset the uncollected difference for that year.

---

1. Katie McKellar, "'Horrific' typo valued Wasatch County home at almost $1 billion," *Deseret News*, December 5, 2019, https://www.deseret.com.

over a 15,000% jump from 1700. Within these figures, the United States has the highest GDP of any country. While we do have economic disparity, the poorest of our poor would still be remarkably wealthier than the poor in Christ's day. But it's more than that. Behind those numbers lies a free-market economy grounded in a democratic state whose socioeconomic, political, and cultural philosophies tout a relatively classless society where education and opportunity abound. This translates to a poverty that, in the main, has significantly more correlation to poor choices. There are certainly exceptions to this broad observation, but generally speaking, an American adult wields incredible control over his material outcome in life.

This was not the case with the poor in Christ's day. The truly indigent were not poor because of bad choices; it was their lot in life. They didn't necessarily lack skill, gift, or talent, but they had no opportunity to put them to use. They were born into poverty and would live and die in it with no ability or hope of extricating themselves. There were no safety nets or welfare, just a long history of inheriting and bequeathing privation from generation to generation. This still exists in some societies today. To think of scolding the slum resident for his irresponsibility would be absurd. To be sure, the abysmal stench of hopeless despair can create a pernicious atmosphere in which sin festers, but by and large their miserable circumstances are not a result of their choices.

In fact, this poverty may often facilitate a humbleness in heart as well. The two can be directly related. The similar Sermon on the Plain recorded in Luke simply states, "Blessed are you who are poor" (Luke 6:20). Quoting D.A. Carson, Craig Blomberg notes that they are "those who because of sustained economic privation and social distress have confidence only in God."[4] Having nowhere and no one else to turn to, they are driven to God as He uses their poverty as a means by which

---

4. Craig Blomberg, *Matthew*, ed. David S. Dockery, vol. 22, *New American Commentary* (Nashville: Broadman Press, 1992), 98.

to draw them to Himself: "He raises the poor from the dust and lifts the needy from the ash heap" (Ps. 113:7). Their desperate condition in one respect can shed light on their desperate condition in another. The contemporary poor in wealthier nations, though, tend to be inoculated against such a response simply because government and other entities make provision for their needs.

Paul observed the correlation when he reminded the church at Corinth:

> For consider your calling, brethren, that there were not many wise according to the flesh, not many mighty, not many noble; but God has chosen the foolish things of the world to shame the wise, and God has chosen the weak things of the world to shame the things which are strong, and the base things of the world and the despised God has chosen, the things that are not, so that He may nullify the things that are, so that no man may boast before God. But by His doing you are in Christ Jesus, who became to us wisdom from God, and righteousness and sanctification, and redemption, so that, just as it is written, "Let him who boasts, boast in the Lord." (1 Cor. 1:26-31)

Likewise, in the context of addressing partiality, James rhetorically admonished the Jewish believers, "Did not God choose the poor of this world to be rich in faith and heirs of the kingdom which He promised to those who love Him?" (James 2:5) God is by no means promising that every poor person will follow after Him. We must be careful to neither commend nor attribute virtue to poverty in and of itself. Pursuing poverty misses the point because the real issue lies in the nature of our hearts. Poverty cannot procure or merit salvation, but it can often produce a humble spirit. Like many axiomatic truths in Proverbs, it upholds a general pattern in life that Scripture affirms.

Within this specific context, America is at a marked disadvantage as the gospel is readily "veiled to those who are perishing, in whose case the god of this world has blinded the minds of the unbelieving so that they might not see the light of the gospel of the glory of Christ, who is the image of God" (2 Cor. 4:3–4). We are rich with so much provision that another obstacle to salvation is placed before us. God still uses His Word by the power of the Holy Spirit to overcome any hurdle, but every single person, regardless of his material wealth, must recognize his own spiritual emptiness in order to gain entrance into the kingdom. Believers continue to reflect this humility to an even greater degree within the kingdom as we increasingly learn more of God's greatness and our overall insignificance by comparison.

As mentioned, our church engages in door-to-door evangelism in our town. We committed to visit every home in our community at least once to share the gospel of Jesus Christ. By His grace we have done so, and throughout the years we witnessed a pattern emerge. Over and over again, the lower-income neighborhoods demonstrated a much higher degree of interest in listening to and engaging with our message. This didn't necessarily mean they responded as the poor in Jesus' time, unfortunately, but we did find that opportunities to preach the gospel dramatically dropped as we moved outside of these areas.

In nicer neighborhoods, it was harder to find people at home. If they were, they were less likely to answer the door, or if they did, they barely gave us the time of day. Typically citing busyness as the excuse to curtail the conversation, they assured us they had everything they needed and politely but quickly shut their doors. As always, exceptions abound, but this has unquestionably been the trend. The Bible in no way denounces wealth in and of itself, nor indicts those who are wealthy; but Scripture does condemn acting rich in heart (1 Tim. 6:17–19). This attitude often accompanies material wealth. They are intelligent, successful, and independent; they know what they need and have met those needs on their own. Trusting in themselves, they ignore the message. While Christ affirmed "with God all things are possible" (Matt. 19:26), He also observed that "it is hard for a rich man to enter the kingdom of heaven" (v. 23).

Those Who Recognize Their Bankruptcy

Now that we've established a relationship between physical and spiritual poverty, we need to further define what it truly means to be "poor in spirit." They are those who have fully recognized their spiritual capital amounts to zero—absolutely nothing. They grasp that they lack the resources necessary to enter the kingdom. Understanding that they cannot receive the favor of God on their own, they acknowledge they're in no position to even borrow; they have no credit, nor do they deserve any. In an act of total self-abandonment, they cast off any trust in themselves and declare utter moral bankruptcy. *While that's a bad place to be materially, it's a great place to be spiritually.* They recognize their sin as a violation against the holy God that deserves eternal punishment: "To be poor in spirit is not to lack courage but to acknowledge spiritual bankruptcy. It confesses one's unworthiness before God and utter dependence on him."[5]

Luke 18 offers a visceral picture of this. While this illustration describes entrance into the kingdom, it still represents the attitude that must pervade our thinking while living within it.

> And He also told this parable to some people who trusted in themselves that they were righteous, and viewed others with contempt: "Two men went up into the temple to pray, one a Pharisee and the other a tax collector. The Pharisee stood and was praying this to himself: 'God, I thank You that I am not like other people: swindlers, unjust, adulterers, or even like this tax collector. I fast twice a week; I pay tithes

---

5. D. A. Carson, *The Expositor's Bible Commentary*, eds. Tremper Longman III and David E. Garland, vol. 9, *Matthew ~ Mark*, (Grand Rapids: Zondervan, 2010), 132.

of all that I get.' But the tax collector, standing some distance away, was even unwilling to lift up his eyes to heaven, but was beating his breast, saying, 'God, be merciful to me, the sinner!' I tell you, this man went to his house justified rather than the other; for everyone who exalts himself will be humbled, but he who humbles himself will be exalted." (Luke 18:9–14)

Two men came to God's holy temple to pray, and the similarities, it seemed, ended there. Christ chose men from incredibly different backgrounds for His parable. From the world's eyes, He chose the most religious and the most contemptible. The Pharisee was the spiritual leader of the day, outwardly holy but trusting in himself. Christ mentioned that he prayed "to himself," which indicated where his confidence lay. The Pharisee recounted all of the reasons his life merited eternal reward in God's presence, both by pointing to his good deeds and comparing himself with others. While this scorekeeping may seem a bit crude, it reveals the heart of the unbeliever who naturally appraises himself. He judges by every standard but God's. "I'm a caring person," the neighbor on his doorstep may say. "I'm well-intended, and I don't wish people harm. I have my life together, and I try to do good things for people. Hell is for others — the really bad people who aren't like me."

Sadly, even believers can harbor echoes of this kind of attitude. We subtly begin to imagine that somehow we warranted our salvation; we must have demonstrated some relative value, we think, that placed us above people who we deem are truly evil. The thought of *I would never do that* insidiously creeps into our minds, and we begin to swell in arrogance once again. Instead, we should practice the spirit of the publican who, in recognizing his true status as a sinner, could only cry out to God to withhold the judgment he rightfully deserved.

Christ's point was not so much about looks being deceiving but that the condition of the heart is what ultimately matters. No one partakes of Christ's righteousness until he fully understands he is bereft of any himself. This lowly mindset should grow as we live in the kingdom, informing our conduct and character. We recognize that we're still nothing apart from what God in His greatness has accomplished within us. He justifies and sanctifies us by His power as we now strive to obey His commands. When we enter His kingdom with poorness of spirit and then revert to arrogance in everything else, we fail to represent our Savior well. We swell with pride even in our spiritual endeavors. Instead, we must cultivate a poorness of spirit that thwarts our sinful flesh's proclivity to think we can retain God's favor on our own. As we continually wrestle, confess, and repent, we point to His greatness.

Those Who Recognize Their Unworthiness

Relatedly, the poor in spirit perceive their own unworthiness. We have all "sinned and fall[en] short of the glory of God" (Rom. 3:23). We do not deserve any blessing. Job eventually recognized this. Over and over, he cried out to God in the midst of his great misery, wondering why he had been thus afflicted. Chapter after chapter his flawed advisors roundly accused him of hidden sin that incited this smiting by God, but finally God shut all of their mouths, including Job. God launched into His own interrogation, rhetorically demanding to know where Job was when He was demonstrating His greatness in creation. Job's reply? "I retract, and I repent in dust and ashes" (Job 42:6). Recognizing he was undeserving of any blessing, Job was obliterated by the worthiness of God.

Sinners *must* have this attitude in order to enter the kingdom, but how often do we maintain this mindset? We tend to drift into a feeling that we deserve blessing when God's unmerited grace is the only reason we have anything. Like Job, we must remember who we truly are and who God truly is. God declares:

> For thus says the high and exalted One
> Who lives forever, whose name is Holy,

"I dwell on a high and holy place,
And also with the contrite and lowly of spirit
In order to revive the spirit of the lowly
And to revive the heart of the contrite." (Isa. 57:15)

The truly contrite repent of thinking that they're something when they're actually nothing, especially when estimating themselves in light of someone who's greater. Considering myself fairly athletic, I was excited for fellowship and confident of victory when my mentor invited me to play racquetball. Though the game was new to me, I expected to handily surpass him once acclimated. Even after our first week of games, all of which I lost 21–0 and resulted in imprints of my face all over the court's walls, I remained bullish on my chances of an impending victory.

After the first *year* of losses, managing only once to score ten points, my pride was finally punctured. Experiencing the position of "loser" was incredibly beneficial in both dealing with the sinful anger that had risen up in my heart and overcoming my inclination to pout and quit when I couldn't win. Just as I needed to humbly admit the reality that he was a better player, how much more must we prostrate ourselves before a holy and perfect God who is infinitely beyond us.

God desires to be with those whose lowly spirits need reviving. He in turn provides what we need to lift us up. We don't have to be concerned with exalting ourselves or demonstrating our worth to others. We simply come to Him naked and needy, first for life and then for living.

Those Who Recognize Their Dependence

Right after Christ shared the parable of the Pharisee and the publican in Luke 18, Jesus began to receive many babies that the crowds were bringing to Him. When the disciples rebuked the people, Jesus corrected them: "Permit the children to come to Me, and do not hinder them, for the kingdom of God belongs to such as these. Truly I say to you, whoever does not receive the kingdom of God like a child will not enter it at all" (Luke 18:16–17). The child's innocence was not the issue, but rather his dependence. There is no better picture of complete and utter dependence than a human baby. As babies cannot in any way survive on their own, so we too must cry out to God for salvation. Babies understand they must rely on someone else and simply turn to receive provision. When hunger for sustenance arises, a baby does not go into the kitchen and cook. Rather, he screams and cries because he knows he doesn't have what he needs, but another does. This similar attitude of reliance on God must continue in sanctified kingdom living. He constantly supplies us with the spiritual resources we need to pursue, love, know, and grow in Him. Just as children can't care for themselves in an ongoing manner, we must constantly turn to God in daily prayer to supply us with each day's grace and provision needed.

Those Who Submit to God's Word

King Josiah was only eight years old when he ascended the throne of Judah after his wicked father was assassinated. The book of 2 Kings introduces him as one who "did right in the sight of the LORD and walked in all the way of his father David, nor did he turn aside to the right or to the left" (22:2). As he commissioned repairs on the badly damaged temple eighteen years into his reign, the high priest discovered God's Word that had been lost in the rubble. Recovering it, they read it, and "when the king heard the words of the book of the law, he tore his clothes" (22:11). Through a prophetess, God told the king: "Because your heart was tender and you humbled yourself before God when you heard His words against this place and against its inhabitants, and because you humbled yourself before Me, tore your clothes and wept before Me, I truly have heard you" (2 Chron. 34:27).

I named my son after this godly king because I prayerfully hoped he would have a similar response to God's Word. By the Lord's grace, he has, as every believer must in order to gain admission into the kingdom. At salvation, we come to the end of ourselves, recognizing our "total spiritual destitution" — our "pride is gone, [our] self-assurance is gone, and [we] stand empty-handed before God."[6] Not only must we retain this heartfelt attitude as kingdom citizens, but it should also be growing.

It's important to note that poorness of spirit is *not* morbid introspection, but God-fearing subjection to His Word. As the sinful flesh tends to pervert everything it encounters, this self-centered introversion "reinforc[es] our natural self-absorption and exacerbat[es] our problems."[7] We are consumed within ourselves rather than looking to God in our personal examinations. Even the phrase "I'm just really hard on myself" is rife with pride, implying we expected better and only feel shame for not representing ourselves as impressively as we hoped. For the believer, an attitude that mulls over past sins and regrets belittles Christ's sacrifice. These protracted bouts of self-focus can quickly descend into self-pity and even a victimized mindset if left unchecked. The Psalms provide excellent examples of combatting this tendency by speaking truth to ourselves, cherishing and obeying His Word, and looking to God, knowing He also searches our hearts (Ps. 139:1).

God reveals, "But to this one I will look, to him who is humble and contrite of spirit, and who trembles at My word" (Isa. 66:2). Within the kingdom, the believer's longing to respond to the Word in faith and obedience increasingly expands. As Christ declared to the

---

6. John MacArthur, *Matthew 1-7*, vol. 1, *The MacArthur New Testament Commentary* (Chicago: Moody Press, 1985), 146.

7. Jared Mellinger, "Look Up: Trading Introspection for Awe," Desiring God, October 4, 2017, https://www.desiringgod.org/articles/look-up.

tempter, we live on "EVERY WORD THAT PROCEEDS OUT OF THE MOUTH OF GOD" (Matt. 4:4). With the psalmist, our hearts sing:

> I have rejoiced in the way of Your testimonies,
> As much as in all riches.
> I will meditate on Your precepts
> And regard Your ways.
>
> My soul is crushed with longing
> After Your ordinances at all times.
>
> I opened my mouth wide and panted,
> For I longed for Your commandments.
> (Ps. 119:14–15; 20; 131)

The believer's growth in humility of heart enables him to serve, honor, and find his ultimate satisfaction in God alone.

Demonstrating Poorness of Spirit

In Thomas Watson's book on the Beatitudes, the seventeenth-century puritan gave seven markers from which to examine one's heart for this inner attitude of humility.[8] Please slowly and thoughtfully consider these demonstrations of spiritual poverty Watson listed:

1. *"He that is poor in spirit is weaned from himself."*[9] Our natural default is for our entire lives to revolve around ourselves. Whether our self-appraisal is high or low, we are still consumed with ourselves, whether lamenting or rejoicing. But the Christian has been rescued from this attachment. As believers grow in the

---

8. Thomas Watson, *The Beatitudes: An Exposition of Matthew 5:1-12*, ed. Anthony Uyl (Woodstock, Ontario, 2017), 19-21.
9. All direct quotations within this list, aside from the parenthetically cited Scripture, belong to Watson.

kingdom, they are increasingly "divorced from themselves." We understand to a greater degree the reality that, if left to ourselves, we would've wound up in eternal hell. We die daily to ourselves, echoing Paul's declaration: "I have been crucified with Christ; and it is no longer I who live, but Christ lives in me; and the life which I now live in the flesh I live by faith in the Son of God, who loved me and gave Himself up for me" (Gal. 2:20).

2. *"He that is poor in spirit is a Christ-admirer."* We came poor, naked, and hungry and found the "unfathomable riches of Christ" at salvation (Eph. 3:8). But as we grow in Him, we continually accumulate "the wealth that comes from the full assurance of understanding, resulting in a true knowledge of God's mystery, that is, Christ Himself, in whom are hidden all the treasures of wisdom and knowledge" (Col. 2:2–3). We continue to cling to Christ for our every breath. He is our "living water" and "bread of life" (John 4:10; 6:35), a storehouse that "can never be emptied."

3. *"He that is poor in spirit is ever complaining of his spiritual estate."* In this sense, Watson meant that we are ever more aware of what we lack in and of ourselves. As a dependent beggar has no resources of his own upon which to draw to sustain himself, so too believers can only come to God and communicate their every need: "The poor in spirit, who have lain all their lives at the gate of mercy and have lived upon the alms of free grace, have died rich in faith, heirs to a kingdom." This disposition of character progresses into mourning, meekness, and hungering and thirsting after righteousness, which we will discuss in the coming chapters.

4. *"He that is poor in spirit is lowly in heart. . . . When he acts most like a saint, [he] confesses himself the 'chief of sinners.'"* With an attitude that cuts against the grain of our former identity, the poor are submissive. The world, perhaps America in particular, scoffs at

such a mindset that rolls itself "in the dust in the sense of [its] unworthiness." Yet with Job, we repent "in dust and ashes" (Job 42:6). Far from being a self-absorbed lament of "woe is me," we exult in others' strengths in light of our own weaknesses. How often do we praise God for the evidence of grace in fellow believers? God's grace humbles us as we ever more clearly see what debtors we are to His grace (Rom. 8:12). We pursue sanctification "strengthened with all power, according to His glorious might" (Col. 1:11), knowing "it is God who is at work in [us], both to will and to work for His good pleasure" (Phil. 2:13).

5. *"He who is poor in spirit is much in prayer."* As we appraise ourselves more accurately, we beg God for grace where we lack holiness. Prayer is the expression of our utter dependence on Him and the means by which we receive the power to accomplish the work He has for us to do. We cry out to God for "more conformity to Christ." Like the persistent widow with the judge, we "at all times . . . ought to pray and not to lose heart" (Luke 18:1). As a beggar is always occupied by begging, the believer "knocks at heaven-gate; he sends up sighs; he pours out tears; he will not away from the gate till he have his dole."

6. *"The poor in spirit is content to take Christ upon [His] own terms."* Christ is not just Savior, but King. He rules over His kingdom. Just as a besieged fortress depleted of every resource is ready to surrender on all the victor's terms in order to live, believers who surrendered to Christ now live by His decrees. When we grow in perceiving our need, we are willing to "behead [our] beloved sin." We understand that His terms are benevolent and of the highest benefit to us.

7. *"He that is poor in spirit is an exalter of free grace."* Believers are characterized by their gratitude. They are ceaselessly thankful for His abundant grace: "None so magnify mercy as the poor in

spirit." Just as a guilty, condemned man suddenly receives an undeserved, merciful pardon, the believer leaps for joy to worship the One who bestowed such mercy. We should be daily praising God for His great grace. Such thanksgiving abounds in Scripture, and we ought to be joining the chorus. Living in the kingdom with a poorness of spirit, we "bless God for the least crumb that falls from the table of free grace." As "poverty of spirit is the foundation stone on which God lays the superstructure of glory," it's also the basis from which the other beatitudes will build.

The Reward

Christ promised blessing to those kingdom citizens who are poor in spirit. The reward of the kingdom is itself. While every other beatitude is a promised future blessing, the first and last beatitudes are recorded by Matthew in the present tense: "for theirs is the kingdom of heaven" (5:3, 10). *This means that even though the kingdom itself isn't fully realized yet, citizens are fully in the kingdom* — a cause for rejoicing indeed. After adopting our two girls from Haiti, we petitioned the government to grant them U.S. citizenship. In the interim, even though they were part of our family, as legal residents they did not have full rights or even a guarantee to stay permanently in the country until citizenship was finalized. They were on the path to citizenship, but they weren't naturalized yet. What a blessing to know that even though Christ has yet to return to usher in the final phases of His kingdom, we are already permanent, full-fledged citizens.

Our path to kingdom citizenship required poorness of spirit to enter through salvation, but this same humility becomes the kingdom's very currency. As we maintain a poorness of spirit, we become spiritually rich. Unlike the church in Laodicea who failed to appraise her state accurately, Christ assured the church at Smyrna: "I know your tribulation and your poverty (but you are rich)" (Rev. 2:9). God desires that we "recognize our lowliness so that He can raise us up."[10] He who possesses all riches is not stingy, but "will supply all [our] needs according to His riches in glory in Christ Jesus" (Phil. 4:19). Outside of Christ, unbelievers have nothing but their own paltry, decrepit kingdoms that are as foul as the deepest, darkest, dankest dungeon. While they think they're ruling, their kingdoms are ultimately controlled by the "spiritual forces of wickedness in the heavenly places" (Eph. 6:12). As believers, we must actively crush the indwelling sin that desires to return to our own puny, crumbling kingdoms. By His grace, we can instead correctly assess the infinite superiority of Christ's realm: "In giving up their own kingdom, the poor in spirit inherit God's."[11]

~

Blest are the humble souls that see
their emptiness and poverty;
treasures of grace to them are giv'n,
and crowns of joy laid up in heav'n.

~Isaac Watts, 1709

---

10. John MacArthur, *Matthew 1–7*, vol. 1, *The MacArthur New Testament Commentary* (Chicago: Moody Press, 1985), 151.
11. MacArthur, *Matthew* (1985), 151.

Questions for Discussion & Reflection

1. Define "poor in spirit."

2. What is the relationship between physical poverty and spiritual poverty?

3. Living in a wealthy society presents what sort of obstacle(s) to grasping both of these kinds of poverty?

4. Describe the "poorness of spirit" demonstrated in your personal testimony of salvation (entrance into the kingdom).

5. How can knowing God better increase our humility while living in the kingdom?

6. Instead of growing as it should, our poorness of spirit in the kingdom can sometimes decline after our admission into it. Why is that, and how can we combat it?

7. What is "morbid introspection"? What can it lead to? How can we guard against it?

8. What reward does Christ offer for those who are poor in spirit?

9. Why do you think poorness of spirit will be the foundation upon which the following beatitudes will build?

Chapter 3

Blessed Are Those Who Mourn

Blessed are those who mourn, for they shall be comforted.

Throughout the years, a tradition emerged from our church's youth camping trips. We would cap off the week with a visit to a local theme park. The reason, far from complex, was twofold—I planned the camps, and I enjoyed a lifetime affinity for these oases of fun. Thankfully, the kids were always happy to accommodate. On recent trips, I've leisurely meandered through the parks with my family, enjoying various rides here and there with no real sense of urgency—this had not always been the case.

In Southern California, amusement parks are almost as common as Costcos. Growing up there, my friends and I would prepare well in advance for our youth group's outings. We would carefully strategize and calculate how to fully utilize a park to optimize our enjoyment. Once the gates swung open, we'd make a deliberate beeline to the rear of the park for the biggest and best rides. With empty lines and attendants just waiting, the rides seemed equally as eager to thrill their first passengers as we were to ride them. Then, we would methodically work our way back to the entrance, racing from ride to ride. The plan was brilliant, but if anything thwarted even a step, we'd be in utter agony. A moment couldn't be spared. There was simply too much fun to be had! At the end of the day, we would drop into our beds absolutely exhausted from our pleasure-seeking.

Is it wrong to run around a theme park like that? Generally, it isn't, but unfortunately, it provides a poignant illustration of how humanity spends their entire lives. From birth to death, they rush around trying to seek, maximize, and prolong their pleasures. They frantically scurry from place to place, squeezing any hope of happiness out of the sinful idols they so desperately crave. Apart from Christ, men can only find gratification in their sin that is limited, perverted, and fleeting. The best may aim high, but even those noble endeavors are deemed "filthy garments" since corrupted hearts direct them (Isa. 64:6).

The kingdom of God, on the other hand, is chiefly characterized by *true* joy. Blessings abound; in fact, the defining feature of kingdom citizenship is fullness of God's pleasures. Believers are fully satisfied in Him, rejoicing over the peace and contentment He alone brings. The Beatitudes that Christ recounted are rich blessings empowered by the Spirit that bring untold pleasures. They are only discovered by those who recognize the evilness of their sin. Instead of embracing it, they greatly mourn over it. *Kingdom citizens possess a fundamental attitude of mourning and weeping over sin.*

The first beatitude promised happiness to those who are poor of spirit. The blessings will begin to build in progression, starting with this second benefit which flows out of the first. As we believers recognize our spiritual bankruptcy, that we have nothing to offer God and stand before Him destitute and unworthy, we will appraise our sin in all its wickedness and greatly mourn over it. In his treatment of the Beatitudes, John Stott observed this transition from the first beatitude to the next: "This is the second stage of spiritual blessing. It is one thing to be spiritually poor and acknowledge it; it is another to grieve and to mourn over it."[1] Kingdom citizens humble themselves beneath God's Word. As we enter the kingdom in this manner, we will remain in that dependent state. If we accurately appraise our lack of any spiritual capital, there will be grief over and hatred for everything in us that violates the character and nature of God.

Defining Mourning

What is *mourning* exactly? In this Beatitude, Jesus essentially declared, "Happy are the sad." What does that mean? How could anything be "more self-contradictory than the idea that the sad are happy, that the path to happiness is sadness, that the way to rejoicing is in mourning"?[2] Such a statement negates the world's beckoning to constantly chase after happiness. Sadness is considered an intruder to be avoided at all costs — an unwelcome anomaly that must be eradicated. This beatitude is as paradoxical as the first. The humble and lowly will actually gain admission into the most illustrious dominion, and the blessed lamenters will be happy in comfort.

Furthermore, just as poorness of spirit can often arise from actual physical poverty, so too can this mourning relate to a real grief over the difficult, physical circumstances in life. But it's more than that. *The popular idea that those who endure a hard life will naturally be rewarded in the end is patently false.* That intuitive thinking is akin to Eastern mysticism, and it's manifestly untrue. Suffering here does not automatically guarantee bliss in the life to come. That's not God's understanding of fairness. In fact, if one only mourns externally, bewailing the trials

---

1. John R. W. Stott, *The Message of the Sermon on the Mount*, rev. ed. (Downers Grove: Intervarsity Press, 2020), 24.
2. John MacArthur, *Matthew 1–7*, vol. 1, *The MacArthur New Testament Commentary* (Chicago: Moody Press, 1985), 153.

of life and not confessing his own sinfulness before a holy God, he will receive nothing but righteous judgment. The afflictions in his life on earth will pale in comparison to those of eternal hell. Christ is not giving everyone assurance that things will be better later if they're suffering now; rather, He is referencing a sincere, spiritual sorrow that recognizes sin's violation against God's perfect character.

True mourning is an internal anguish over sin, experienced by true believers as they both embrace Scripture's teaching on the evilness of sin and willfully determine to properly deal with it. John MacArthur frames it this way:

> The faithful child of God is constantly broken over his sinfulness, and the longer he lives and the more mature he becomes in the Lord, the harder it is for him to be frivolous. He sees more of God's love and mercy, but he also sees more of his own and the world's sinfulness. To grow in grace is also to grow in the awareness of sin.[3]

By "frivolous," he is referencing this foolish happiness the world recklessly pursues, in spite of rampant sin ravaging their lives and the lives of everyone around them. Believers, by contrast, do not treat sin lightly. We appropriately mourn as a response to recognizing our spiritual bankruptcy. Before delving into the characteristics of true mourners, though, let's first briefly examine some inappropriate responses to sin.

Improper Mourning

The Pharisees failed to mourn altogether. Since they simply denied any spiritual bankruptcy in the first place, mourning was rendered

---

3. MacArthur, *Matthew* (1985), 159.

unnecessary. Although Scripture was clear, they practiced the very things they judged, but denied their guilt before a holy God (Rom. 2:1). As their consciences (and Christ!) no doubt convicted them internally, they fiercely clung to their external self-righteousness all the more, convinced that it made them good enough. This can be an unbeliever's response to sin, but it can even be functionally mimicked by believers at times. We don't want to be confronted with our wickedness, so we just press harder into manufacturing righteousness. We pretend to be spiritual millionaires when we are actually spiritual paupers.

Or perhaps our response might more closely resemble an ascetic, someone who practices strict self-denial. Such people may recognize their shortcomings but try to atone for them by intentionally making their own lives hard. Such penance accomplishes nothing. No scales are balanced.

Similarly, monks in monasteries also made their lives purposely difficult, but they primarily focused on external evils. They removed themselves from the world. Renouncing it, they sought their purity and holiness through isolation and simplicity. There's been a resurgence of this idea trending in some Christian circles, but it ultimately accomplishes nothing. Attempts to escape from the world fail to eradicate the sin residing in the heart. People merely take their sinful hearts with them. It doesn't matter where they go. Christ pointed out: "But the things that proceed out of the mouth come from the heart, and those defile the man. For out of the heart come evil thoughts, murders, adulteries, fornications, thefts, false witness, slanders" (Matt. 15:18–19).

Some may take a different approach entirely. They recognize their spiritual poverty but remain in despair over it. They may drown their sorrow in drink, drugs, or illicit activities. Others may completely withdraw in utter hopelessness by taking their own lives as Judas did (Matt. 27:5). They assumed that because they couldn't find a satisfactory solution, there wasn't one.

We can mourn over our sin improperly in other ways. Sometimes we grieve because we simply don't get what we want. We mourn over our own unmet desires. This grief is akin to Amnon's unfulfilled sexual longing for a member of his own family. He grew "so frustrated because of his sister Tamar that he made himself ill, for she was a virgin, and it seemed hard to Amnon to do anything to her" (2 Sam. 13:2). In this example, Amnon's sinful grief manifested itself physically. While we may not necessarily be sinfully lusting after an unlawful relationship, we can inordinately desire good and right things to the point of idolatry. Maybe we want the perfect marriage or a happy family with God-fearing children who grow up and establish their lives around us. If that doesn't happen, we inappropriately grieve over our thwarted aspirations rather than our own idolatrous hearts. There's no blessing promised in this selfish mourning over sinful idol-grasping that supplants Christ's supremacy.

Mourning to a sinful extreme is also inappropriate. When we recognize our sin, sometimes we become fixated on it, and our grief takes over in an unhealthy and ungodly way. We wallow in our sin. People call this "beating themselves up," but it's just arrogantly refusing to accept God's forgiveness. It flows out of the sorrow that painful consequences from sin produce. There are clearly weighty circumstances through which we must wrestle and respond rightly. But if we allow ourselves to be consumed with regret, we will grow embittered and refuse to take hold of God's greatness in delivering us from every sin through Christ's provision. Sinclair Ferguson points out that true mourning

> is emphatically not to be equated with a heavy and depressive spirit. Some of us by nature are melancholic, and sink more easily in our spirits. We become introverted and develop a poor image of ourselves, . . . [but those] can be characteristics of a person who is absorbed in himself; rather than is poor in spirit. By contrast, the man who genuinely mourns

because of his sin has been drawn out of himself to see God in his holiness and grace. It is this—his sight of God—that has made him mourn.[4]

David exemplified this immoderate mourning in the death of his son Absalom. Attempting to overthrow his father, Absalom sought to kill David. He desired to usurp the throne of God's appointed king. David's military clashed with his son's, and his commander Joab came across Absalom and killed him, in spite of David's explicit command to leave him unharmed: "The king charged Joab . . . saying, 'Deal gently for my sake with the young man Absalom'" (2 Sam. 18:5). When the king heard the news, he lamented and wept bitterly. Instead of rejoicing in victory over those who dared to challenge God and depose His chosen leader, the people of Jerusalem witnessed David unduly agonize over the traitor's death. How was David bemoaning his son's death sinfully improper?

Clearly, he anguished over his own sin that ultimately caused Absalom's downfall. It could be traced all the way back to that day he decided to stay home from battle and scope out the nearby rooftops. After David committed adultery with Bathsheba and had her godly husband killed, God promised that "the sword shall never depart from [David's] house" (12:10). David seemed to dwell so constantly on this pronouncement, he was overcome with regret and failed to embrace what was right and good. In fact, Joab directly reproved him, explaining that David was hating those who loved him by loving those who hated him (2 Sam. 19:1–7). He warned the king that if he didn't respond properly, his reign would come to an abrupt end. By the Lord's grace, David repented. Likewise, if our children who love us pass away, we cannot allow our proper lamentation to cross over into sinful excess or be bound up in ungodly regret over past sin.

Neither must our mourning soothe our own egos. Sometimes we bewail our sin that causes others to no longer perceive us in the way

---

4. Sinclair Ferguson, *The Sermon on the Mount* (Banner of Truth, 1988), 11–24.

we desire. Our reputations are adversely impacted, and we grieve our humiliation. King Saul demonstrated this when he disobeyed God by failing to entirely destroy the Amalekites and their livestock. Samuel confronted Saul, who denied any disobedience. When pressed further, he admitted his transgression stemmed from "fear[ing] the people and listen[ing] to their voice" (1 Sam. 15:24). He still justified his half-hearted confession by claiming he aimed to please God by offering the spared livestock as sacrifices to Him. Trying to convince the prophet to return with him to "worship," the underlying motive slipped out: Saul repined, "I have sinned; but please honor me now before the elders of my people and before Israel, and go back with me" (v. 30). He wanted to hold onto the kingship and the praise of men it brought. Saul deplored his disobedience, but it was the worldly sorrow of false repentance that he carried for the rest of his life.

Proper Mourning

How do we mourn properly? The right response more closely approximates the prodigal son who admitted his condition, grieved over it, and turned to his father for the remedy (Luke 15:11–32). This is a true mourning over our personal sin against a holy God. When we recognize our evilness in light of His character, it causes great anguish that isn't bound up in ego or idol. It is born out of a love for God.

Physical Anguish

In fact, it's sufficiently weighty to bring physical affliction in some cases. We can return to David as our example; this time, as a commendation rather than a warning. In Psalm 32, David cried out:

> When I kept silent about my sin, my body wasted
> away
> Through my groaning all day long.

For day and night Your hand was heavy upon me;
My vitality was drained away as with the fever
heat of summer. (vv. 3–4)

Though David didn't remain here, he began here. Because he first rightly perceived the gravity of his sin, he then learned to confess it, exclaiming:

How blessed is he whose transgression is forgiven,
Whose sin is covered!
How blessed is the man to whom the Lord does not
impute iniquity,
And in whose spirit there is no deceit! (vv. 1–2)

His words parallel the Beatitude. While David should have dealt with the unconfessed sin before his body was ravaged by it, we observe how the heinous nature of sin can cause a visceral reaction within us. Believers *must* deal with their sin through confession and repentance; they cannot hold onto it without severe implications. By contrast, many unbelievers feel no such weight, even those who profess Christ as their Lord.

Internal Discord

Unhappily, within two different churches in which I grew up, pastors had long-term affairs with their secretaries and, judging by their statements and subsequent conduct, appeared more bothered by being exposed than by the vile nature of their wickedness. Both maintained their professions of faith all the way out the door, but where was the internal anguish tormenting and crushing them over their ongoing and unconfessed sin? Why weren't they overwhelmed by the rank hypocrisy of shepherding a flock while engaging in such evil behavior? While we must be careful to properly evaluate the subjective, mutable feelings of our own hearts, a component of emotional incongruity can certainly mark true mourning. David fleshed this out in another Psalm: "For I know my transgressions, and my sin is ever before me" (51:3). David experienced the dissonance that arose when a true believer harms his relationship with the God he loves. This produces the inner turmoil, not the painful external suffering that may come from sin.

Consequently, proper mourning can serve as a helpful litmus test of kingdom citizenship. Does our sin deeply grieve us because it creates a relational barrier with our loving Father? We can be easily tempted to downplay our sin, or just to avoid thoughts about it altogether. The convenience-driven, amusement-oriented vanity fair in which we live counteracts this hard and necessary reflection by providing myriad distractions and false comforts in which to escape. We can forget all about it. By the Spirit's power, however, as believers grow in sanctification, they increasingly view their sin head-on in all of its ugliness.

Focus on God

True mourning for believers also keeps God front and center. This focus prevents a morbid introspection that inevitably spirals downward into utter despair. David continued,

> Against You, You only, I have sinned
> And done what is evil in Your sight,
> So that You are justified when You speak
> And blameless when You judge. (51:4)

He realized the gravity of his sin because he recognized God's just right to judge his sin. This is crucial because *at any point where we feel vindicated or justified in our sin, we will not properly mourn*. We will make excuses, blame others, compare with others' sins, or even take partial responsibility. But fundamentally we are failing to agree that God is justified when He judges, and our heinous sin against His holiness warrants nothing short of eternal condemnation. Only then will we properly mourn. *In fact, to the extent we acknowledge that God is just in judging our sin will we demonstrate true mourning over it.* In no way are we removing the weightiness of real harm our sin has enacted on others, but by focusing on God, we are confessing that He is the One before whom we are ultimately guilty.

In what areas of life are we taking our sin too lightly and, thus, mitigating our mourning? Do we partially blame our spouse? Our kids? A long-term illness? Difficult circumstances? Difficult people? If we have an excuse, we will fail to fully mourn. This can doubtless prevent unbelievers from entering the kingdom, but it can also greatly hinder believers from experiencing blessedness from within it. Believers must remove the excuses. This doesn't mean people don't tempt, provoke, and even facilitate our sinning. Sometimes they commit abominable sins against us and loved ones: abuse, murder, rape.

These atrocities make it easy to sin, but ultimately, they cannot pardon us from ever violating the character and nature of God. He has made provision! *Infinitely perfect and immeasurably above us, our holy and righteous God graciously and lovingly gave His own Son to die for us, thereby providing a place upon which we can lay down our own wrath against evil – the very spot He poured out His wrath on ours.* He imparts the ability to truly forgive because Christ's sacrifice is fully sufficient. We are without excuse. We must accept full responsibility for our own sin and grow to hate it, knowing that our sin stomps on the very sacrifice Christ so freely offered. That is weighty. That is what should inspire proper mourning.

Rejection of Sin's Pleasures

Rejecting the pleasure of sin is another aspect of true mourning. Surprisingly, the reason we sin is because we like it. As believers, we no doubt experience the Pauline ambivalence of doing what we don't want to do and not doing what we now desire to do (Rom. 7:14–25).

But if we continue in sin, we are choosing that pleasure over the pleasures of serving God. We must recognize that we aren't forced to sin; we choose it. The book of James gives New Testament expression to these Psalms: "Be miserable and mourn and weep; let your laughter be turned into mourning and your joy to gloom" (4:9). This verse is often misunderstood. Within the context, we may think, *I don't laugh over my sin.* He simply means taking pleasure in our sin, and laughter is an expression of our pleasure. It's what the world does; they laugh and wink at foibles and flaws, and James is admonishing the church to stop finding gratification in sin. Instead, it should bring gloom.

Yet even the bitterness, jealousy, or covetousness that we hold in our hearts serve us and provide some level of enjoyment. Otherwise, we would not succumb to these fleshly enticements. We can sinfully prefer them to the joy of forgiveness and contentment. Bitterness, for example, flows out into harmful behavior toward others that we somehow convince ourselves is of benefit to us. According to the Bible, anytime we hold onto these sins and fail to repent, we are taking delight in them. This is grievous evil in the sight of God that should cause us to fall to our knees with profound sorrow.

Abhor Evil

As we learn to rightly mourn over our sin, we will grow to hate it. In Romans 12, as Paul transitioned from the blessings of salvation in God to our response in offering our bodies as living sacrifices, he exhorted: "Let love be without hypocrisy. Abhor what is evil; cling to what is good" (v. 9). Paul employed a very intensive verb in his command. We should not merely try to steer clear of evil or focus on doing enough good to offset it — we should be absolutely repulsed by it, as if it induced a gagging reflex within us. We should shudder at evil, loathing it with every fiber of our being. Imagine if we were tossed headfirst into a manure pile. Horrified, we would extract ourselves immediately, frantically wiping off our faces. That's how we should treat our sin. When sin comes out of our mouths, we should utterly despise it and be deeply grieved by it.

Fearing the Lord is a mark of true believers — the beginning of wisdom (Prov. 9:10); and God equates fearing Him to scorning evil (8:13). When we start to truly hate wickedness, then we will put it away. We will want no more to indulge in it than we want to wallow in that manure pile. We will do everything possible to extricate ourselves; if we don't, that's a symptom we don't hate it enough. When we cultivate a hatred of sin more than merely bemoaning its difficulties, we will learn to fittingly mourn. Often, we develop a hatred of wickedness perpetrated against us, and we weep over the vile harm done in those circumstances, but there's no equal grief over our own sin in the midst of life's trials. J.C. Ryle pointed out that "abhor[ing] our own transgressions is the first symptom of spiritual health."[5] Would that we be quicker to weep over our own sin because we committed it, even if it appears marginal compared to others' offenses! Even though He was completely sinless, Christ wept. Shockingly, His tears were not on the cross from sin's heavy burden or His Father's holy wrath. Rather, He wept at man's sin that brought death for His friend Lazarus.

Willingness to Confess Sin

When we actually abhor our sin because of its vile affront to God and its spurning of Christ's sacrifice, we will want to confess it. We will want to be done with it! If left unaddressed, however, we will continue to clutch it. Perhaps we may offer up false apologies, but there's no true repentance if there's no sincere confession produced by a true mourning. Returning to Psalm 51, David declared:

> Make me to hear joy and gladness,
> Let the bones which You have broken rejoice.

---

5. J. C. Ryle, *Expository Thoughts on the Gospel of Mark*, rev. ed. (Abbotsford, WI: Aneko Press, 2020), 25.

Hide Your face from my sins
And blot out all my iniquities.
Create in me a clean heart, O God,
And renew a steadfast spirit within me. (vv. 8–10)

He cried out to God for forgiveness and deliverance. He begged Him to show lovingkindness, though his sin rightfully incurred God's righteous adjudication. This true repentance is also mentioned by Paul. He expressed to the church at Corinth, "I rejoice not that you were made sorrowful, but that you were made sorrowful to the point of repentance, for you were made sorrowful according to the will of God, so you might not suffer loss in anything through us" (2 Cor. 7:9). The apostle desired that God would use the truth in his letter to produce a true sorrow conforming to God's will that would lead to "repentance without regret" (v. 10).

Sadly, I have counseled many people over the years who have claimed to truly confess and repent. But time revealed a repentance *with* regret for the circumstances in which they found themselves, not true mourning over the offense against God. Excuses began to flood the hollow cavity of false confession. A whole litany of justifications emerged and as the difficult situations tended to improve, their contrition vanished. The fleeting nature of the grief revealed that a proper mourning over sin never occurred. It was a false sorrow. The agony emanated from unmet desires, not God's impugned character. True mourning includes humble confession with a sincere crying out to the Lord.

Mourning Over Others' Sin

As we learn to mourn biblically, it impacts our response to the sins of others as well. If mourning is actually based on God's name being profaned, the sin in the world should cause our hearts to break. In a vision, the prophet Ezekiel beheld God instructing an angel, "Go through the midst of the city, even through the midst of Jerusalem, and put a mark on the foreheads of the men who sigh and groan over all the abominations which are being committed in its midst" (Ezek. 9:4). This visceral grief over the societal decay was not because it made their lives difficult. It was a deep-seated lamentation over the city's depravity that sought to rob God of His due glory. They deplored the wickedness that blasphemed God.

Witnessing our own cultural degeneration, we can be tempted to bewail the devastation and hardship it brings us and our loved ones. Instead, we must grow in our hatred of sin as it is bound up in our love for the Lord. Our hearts ought to resonate with the psalmist: "My eyes shed streams of water, because they do not keep Your law" (119:136). The whole reason for weeping lies in the defilement of God's name. They rebelled against Him and didn't reflect Him. This brought the psalmist to tears, as it should us.

The Reward for Mourning

Appropriately, the corresponding reward for those who mourn is comfort. The happiness arises not from the grief, but from God's response to it. We are blessed beyond measure by the forgiveness God grants to those who rightly mourn over their sin. True joy stems from the comfort found in this bestowed forgiveness. Only those who properly mourn over their sin can access this happiness because their sins are forgiven! Worldly sorrow can never bring comfort because comfort is unattainable without forgiveness—unbelievers are still "dead in their trespasses and sins" (Eph. 2:1). True happiness is beyond their grasp, and "no amount of human effort or optimistic pretense, no amount of positive thinking or possibility thinking, can produce" it—ever.[6]

But when we properly mourn with a true repentance and a trust in God's provision in Christ, the Spirit awakens and rescues our dead

---

6. MacArthur, *Matthew* (1985), 158.

hearts. We enter the kingdom. This divine crescendo of transcendent blessing builds in progression: mourning which brings repentance, which brings forgiveness, which brings comfort, which brings joy. Believers remain joyful and comforted within the kingdom as we continue to recognize our sin and take hold of His forgiveness. Because of his sin, David cried out to God, "Restore to me the joy of Your salvation" (Ps. 51:12). Knowing joy is the culmination of this process, he mourned, admitted, and turned from his sin to find the forgiveness, comfort, and joy God grants. David didn't lose his salvation; believers always possess a constant joy over that security. But his ongoing sin had forfeited a level of contentment experienced by kingdom citizens. He had robbed himself of this cheerfulness by his unrepentant sin, so David returned to godly mourning.

David already anticipated the results that would come from the restoration of joy:

> Then I will teach transgressors Your ways,
> And sinners will be converted to You.
> Deliver me from bloodguiltiness, O God, the God of
> my salvation;
> Then my tongue will joyfully sing of Your
> righteousness.
> O Lord, open my lips,
> That my mouth may declare Your praise. (vv. 13–15)

Are you wrestling with praising and worshiping God? Do you wrestle with ministering to others? With sharing the gospel? Often a lack of mourning over our own sin hinders our fellowship with God. That, in turn, strips the delight from kingdom work. I don't simply order my congregation each week to complete these tasks. They must be motivated to labor for the King because He died for their souls to accomplish this work. He alone is worthy.

When we harbor unmourned sin, there is less comfort and joy. But when we mourn, believers will always find the inexpressible, divine comfort that surpasses any circumstantially driven peace. It is a true comfort whose foundation rests in God's favor through Christ, but as we grow in sanctification, we are also drawn closer to Him in a relational joy through the hatred of sin. The world cannot offer anything remotely akin to this kind of blessed comfort; and it's available to every believer at all times.

This godly comfort finds its ultimate culmination in heaven. God promises believers that "He will wipe away every tear from their eyes; and there will no longer be any death; there will no longer be any mourning or crying or pain" (Rev. 21:4). We tend to think of the suffering here on earth as the pain that will be no more, but what has caused all of that anguish? *Sin.* The primary joy and comfort of heaven is that we will no longer be sinful. We will have no need to mourn because we will not have committed anything over which to mourn! Do we long for that day when sin will be gone forever?

To conclude, here are some practical, actionable steps we can take to mourn properly:

- *Stop loving sin.* Like Moses, choose the riches found in Christ instead of the passing pleasures of sin (Heb. 11:24–26).

- *Stop living in despair.* Set it aside and take hold of God's forgiveness.

- *Stop wallowing in your sinfulness.* This morbid introspection cannot produce true grief.

- *Stop trying to hide your sin out of pride.* Own up to it before God because He's "OPPOSED TO THE PROUD, BUT GIVES GRACE TO THE HUMBLE" (James 4:6).

- *Stop presuming.* Don't presume upon God's grace by continuing in your sin. While His grace is endless, it is only extended to those who humbly recognize their need for it.

- *Stop procrastinating.* Quit saying that you are going to get serious about your sin tomorrow. Don't let the cares of the world and all of your weighty responsibilities distract you. You must make time to mourn over your sin. In reality, you don't have time *not* to mourn. It's that serious.

- *Don't be a Pharisee.* Stop maintaining the irrational delusion that you need to "clean yourself up first" before coming to God. You can't "get it together" before approaching Him. *His* holiness and righteousness clothe you.

- *Study sin.* Do a word study in the Bible on *sin*. Use online resources. Set your mind to study it for a few weeks, and your life will change. Again, you *must* find the time to start hating your sin.

- *Study the holiness of God.* After studying sin, contemplate God's attributes, which work in tandem. Seeing God's exaltedness in light of our own depravity leads to greater grief over sin.

- *Gaze at the cross.* Meditate on it. What exactly did Jesus accomplish? Constantly bring those rich, multifaceted truths to your mind. God's attributes of holiness, justice, wrath, love, mercy, and grace all meet in perfect harmony on the cross in Christ Jesus and His work.

- *Pray.* Set aside significant time to seek the Lord. Cry out to Him to help you recognize, understand, have remorse over, repent from, and recover from your sin.

~

Blest are the men of broken heart,
who mourn for sin with inward smart;
the blood of Christ divinely flows,
a healing balm for all their woes.

~Isaac Watts, 1709

Questions for Reflection & Discussion

1. Make a list of typical idols from which even believers hope to obtain pleasure. Which of the items on the list are you prone to pursue?

2. Many in the world believe those who are afflicted during their life here will find eternal reward for their suffering. What do you think is behind this popular idea? Is it biblical? Why or why not?

3. Define true mourning in the context of this Beatitude. Can unbelievers demonstrate this? Why or why not?

4. What were some examples of improper mourning? Are you tempted to mimic any of them?

5. Keeping in mind this is a helpful litmus test for true kingdom citizenship, does your sin deeply grieve you because it creates a relational barrier with your loving Father?

6. Do you ever feel justified in your sin (i.e, make excuses, minimize your role, etc.)? Where in life do you take sin too lightly by blaming others or circumstances? How can you start combating it today? Is there anyone to whom you need to take ownership of your sin?

7. We are tempted to respond sinfully when sinned against. How are believers enabled to give a pardon instead, even considering the abuse, rape, or murder of a loved one?

8. How much do you hate your sin? Do you long for heaven in part because of its absence? How can you grow to hate it more?

9. Describe examples of the comfort God has given in the midst of your mourning.

10. Pick at least three of the actionable steps from the list at the end of the chapter and put them into practice this month.

Chapter 4

Blessed Are the Gentle

Blessed are the gentle, for they shall inherit the earth.

Born a century before Christ, Gaius Julius Caesar was no stranger to power. Equal parts soldier and politician, he was a brilliant military tactician and savvy political negotiator. Skillfully leveraging both for his own ambitious ends, the calculating general commanded his troops to cross the Rubicon River and seize the heart of the Roman republic. The man for whom every successor was named set up his own empire, desiring to dominate the entire world. An admirer of his Greek predecessor Alexander the Great, Caesar also conquered most of Europe and the Mediterranean, along with portions of Africa, Asia Minor, and the Middle East. But ironically, while seeking to take the world by force, his own life ended in like manner—the power-hungry dictator who famously bragged, "I came, I saw, I conquered," was violently assassinated by self-interested politicians seeking to curb his rule.

His death resulted in an imperial legacy of murder, intrigue, plots, and power plays at the highest levels for centuries, along with a continued pursuit to subjugate the world. Though in the distant past, the idea of exerting force is not at all far removed from us today: ongoing bloodshed in war-torn nations; radicalized mobs looting and rioting in the streets; cartel gangs wreaking havoc on local populations; totalitarian surveillance states crushing their suppressed citizenry; constant fear in societies plagued by violent terrorists; and ethnic conflicts culminating in wholesale genocide. They all reveal that the kingdoms of the world have forever sought to advance by power. This is true even of individuals. Everyone wants to rule his own little kingdom, his own small piece of the world in which he lives out his agenda. It's human nature and has been since the fall.

But this is not how the kingdom of God operates. In fact, God promises that those who are gentle will inherit the earth. Once again, Christ surprised His listeners with a seemingly contradictory statement. Jesus taught that *the kingdom of heaven is not entered into or advanced by forceful assertiveness, but by gentle persistence.* It's the exact opposite of how the world seeks to extend and expand its kingdoms.

Now that we have reached our third Beatitude, they are beginning to build in progression as foreshadowed. We saw how these character traits are necessary not only to enter the kingdom through salvation, but to properly live within it as a believer. We examined the spiritual bankruptcy that must be recognized if we are to live in continual dependence on God. By the Spirit's working, we grow in humility as we perceive to an ever-greater degree who we actually are in relation to Him. Next, we learned this lowliness of heart drives us to properly mourn over our sin. As a result, God blesses us with comfort. This godly grief informs our ongoing repentance and fuels our growing abhorrence of evil. Sin's fleeting pleasures are exchanged for the lavish comfort and joy God delights to bestow on His children.

These first two beatitudes have laid the foundation from which to cultivate a gentle heart. If we are not a pauper and a mourner, we will never be gentle. Instead, we will be forceful, agitated, and selfishly desirous for what *we* want. James 4 addresses this directly:

> What is the source of quarrels and conflicts among you? Is not the source your pleasures that wage war in your members? You lust and do not have; so you commit murder. You are envious and cannot obtain; so you fight and quarrel. (vv. 1–2)

Until we lay aside these sinful desires, we will be unable to demonstrate gentleness and enjoy its promised blessing.

Defining Gentleness

Used only a handful of times in Scripture, the precise meaning of *gentleness* in the Greek is slightly lost in translation. Even with frequent usage in our own lexicon, the word's meaning is still somewhat elusive. Some Bible translations use the even more misunderstood term *meek* in this verse. Unfortunately, our society tends to think of the meek person as a timid wallflower who never speaks up and passively allows others to crush him. It certainly has a connotation of weakness in our culture, but that's neither true meekness nor gentleness.

We are in need of a biblical definition. Lowliness and thoughtfulness underlie the base meaning of the Greek word used in this passage. A gentle person is characterized by a humble heart as opposed to a harsh arrogance. The word signifies a willingly submissive, amenable, and teachable spirit toward God's Word that manifests as genuine selflessness in consideration of others.

In Greek literature, this term was primarily used to describe the harnessing of animals. In a largely agrarian economy, they knew that while strong animals could be useful for farmwork, they needed to be domesticated. That way, their power could be properly channeled for profitable work. If a farmer were to simply turn an ox loose in a field, he would just haphazardly trample the ground. But if the ox's power is suitably harnessed, the entire field can be evenly plowed more efficiently and the crop yield maximized. He becomes incredibly effective. That's the idea behind this word. There's power bound up in the term, but rightly controlled power. It's expended wisely and beneficially. God works this fruit of the Spirit within believers to exercise it in a manner that pleases and honors Him. Unbelievers are incapable of this. They can never wield power appropriately and will eventually wind up abusing it. Lord Acton was correct in observing that "absolute power corrupts absolutely."[1]

Unless we exert power that's properly directed by the Spirit of God, we will never rightly advance the kingdom. Men's arrows miss the mark on either side of the target. Some tend to view gentleness as the art of never offending anyone. One must always be polite and avoid confrontation in any way. Others view it as a wimpy and weak character flaw to be eschewed at all costs. Those who hold to this perspective value power as a virtue unto itself.

So, what is the biblical definition? When confronting the adulterous woman in John 8, Christ graciously rescued her from being stoned to death. He offered her grace but admonished her to forsake sinning: "I do not condemn you, either. Go. From now on sin no more" (v. 12). That's an example of the gentleness of Christ, a proper expression of His directed power. On other occasions, Christ directly confronted the Pharisees. Far from sheepishly asking them not to be so self-righteous, He labeled them hypocrites, widow-devourers, blind guides, fools, lawless, whitewashed tombs, serpents, and a brood of vipers—all in one censorious address (Matt. 23:13–33). Yet His exchanges with the adulterous woman and the Pharisees were both expressions of perfectly exercised gentleness for Him to complete the necessary work

---

1. Lord Acton, "Acton-Creighton Correspondence," 1887, Online Library of Liberty, https://oll.libertyfund.org.

His Father had given Him to do. It was "strength under control, power harnessed in loving service."[2]

Thus, Christ's example defines the concept biblically. *Gentleness is the Holy Spirit-empowered ability to humbly and graciously exercise God's power in just the necessary measure to accomplish His purposes.* It's an attitude of the heart that manifests in conduct:

> Meekness is not cowardice or emotional flabbiness. It is not lack of conviction nor mere human niceness. But its courage, its strength, its conviction, and its pleasantness come from God, not from self. The spirit of meekness is the spirit of Christ, who defended the glory of His Father, but gave Himself in sacrifice for others.[3]

Our poor and mournful hearts qualify us to exercise God's power fittingly to accomplish His kingdom work, never to pursue our own priorities. That's how gentleness works and, as we will see, how the world is gained. The world is conquered, or *inherited*, by this godly gentleness that enables us to properly absorb and exert God's great power to achieve His ends.

Demonstrating Gentleness — God

Gentleness is an attribute of God. The all-powerful, all-knowing, and all-present God is, in fact, gentle. The Bible describes His gentleness, so studying His character will inform the manner in which we likewise will demonstrate this spiritual fruit.

---

2. Timothy George, *Galatians*, vol. 30, *The New American Commentary* (Nashville: Broadman & Holman, 1994), 404.
3. John MacArthur, *Matthew 1–7*, vol. 1, *The MacArthur New Testament Commentary* (Chicago: Moody Press, 1985), 171.

Gently Blowing

The Bible chronicles the incredible account of Elijah and the 450 prophets of Baal. Accepting the prophet's challenge, the pagan priests were unable to successfully call on their god to create fire for their offering. After mocking their fake, powerless deity, Elijah turned to build his own sacrifice. To raise the stakes, he doused the entire altar in water and called upon the Lord to show His people that He alone was God. Fire came down from heaven and consumed the entire sacrifice. The people fell to their faces, and at Elijah's request, rounded up the false prophets for him to justly slay.

Despite this impressive display of God's power, the prophet fled for his life when the king's wife Jezebel vowed to kill him within twenty-four hours. God was patient with Elijah, providing for him and directing him to Mount Horeb where He revealed to him even greater and mightier acts:

> And a great and strong wind was rending the mountains and breaking in pieces the rocks before the LORD; but the LORD was not in the wind. And after the wind an earthquake, but the LORD was not in the earthquake. After the earthquake a fire, but the LORD was not in the fire; and after the fire a sound of a gentle blowing. (1 Kings 19:11–12)

God purposely passed by Elijah in the gentle blowing rather than the awesome demonstrations of power. He wasn't in the gusty gales, ground shaking, or glow of the flames. Yet that's what Elijah had come to expect all of the time. He wanted God to vanquish his adversaries, and Jezebel surely topped that list. While God had sometimes worked in this way, He didn't always. The gentle breeze was not an internal voice inside him, but a physical manifestation like the others to remind Elijah that He expresses His power in the exact amount every moment according to His will. In fact, He often works in quiet, imperceptible ways, but no less effective. We ourselves experience the powerful, yet invisible, impact of the Spirit working the Word within our hearts.

Gently Leading

Isaiah also vividly displays the broad scope of God's gentleness:

> Behold, the Lord GOD will come with might,
> With His arm ruling for Him.
> Behold, His reward is with Him
> And His recompense before Him. (40:10)

Almighty God reigns supreme as sole Sovereign over the universe He created. This book of the Bible is packed with similar testaments to God's greatness. Even in His matchless authority, He never forgets Himself or uses immoderate force. He neither oversteps nor overexerts. The next verse runs to the other end of the spectrum of true gentleness:

> Like a shepherd He will tend His flock,
> In His arm He will gather the lambs
> And carry them in His bosom;
> He will gently lead the nursing ewes. (v. 11)

What a pair of verses! At the same time, God carefully and tenderly provides for those in His care. He always accomplishes the right work in the right manner at the right time with *just* the right measure of power. He always gently leads us with the perfect amount of tenderness and strength. He is never inappropriately rough with His children, and our lives in the kingdom should match that standard.

As a parent, I find this very challenging. When my children were younger, I would discipline as an extension of that mighty arm dispensing divine recompense. But it would be difficult for me to instantly shift to the role of comforter, gently picking them up in my arms to console them. However, if properly executed in my heart, the transition should not be stilted or contrived. God does this perfectly. By His Spirit's power, we too can develop a gentleness that moves and adapts to the contours of every unique situation and relationship, skillfully navigating as the need for levels of gentleness continually fluctuates.

Gently Upholding

In His tender mercy, God cares for us as He gently supports us:

> You have also given me the shield of Your salvation,
> And Your right hand upholds me;
> And Your gentleness makes me great. (Ps. 18:35)

His gentleness enables us to become what He desires us to be. His tender and powerful work in our lives shapes and molds us into His Son's image, providing everything we need for true greatness. He has condescended to protect and sustain us — we who are less than nothing by comparison to His worth and greatness. Yet God warms us, gently tending to our needs even when we grieve Him. Even when His hand is felt to be heavy upon us, we must remember that benevolent, loving hand is always gentle.

Gentle Heart

In the New Testament, Christ came to further reveal the character and nature of God through His life of perfect righteousness. In Matthew 11, He summoned:

> Come to Me, all who are weary and heavy-laden, and
> I will give you rest. Take My yoke upon you and learn
> from Me, for I am *gentle* and humble in heart, and you
> will find rest for your souls. For My yoke is easy and
> My burden is light. (vv. 28–30, emphasis added)

The Greek word that Christ used to describe Himself in this passage is the same He employed in the beatitude. In these verses, Christ tenderly ensured our growth and comfort as we come underneath His authority. We take up our Master's yoke because He's gentle with us. As a result, He enables *us* to be gentle by properly exerting His power to accomplish the work He has for us. We are the beast of burden in this metaphor, guided by our kind, gracious Master.

We were designed to accomplish God's purposes and find our utmost pleasure in pursuing Him and His glory. Christ promises to properly utilize the yoke according to His nature. He would never abuse us or place undue burden on us for which He Himself would not also supply the strength to endure. This life can often be brutal. It may feel as if Christ's yoke is heavy and harsh. When loved ones suffer and die, or when sickness and tragedy strike, it may not seem right, tender, or gentle at all. Yet this is still God's gentle hand; it is never too much, even though it can poignantly feel that way. That's why we cling to these promises from the Word by faith, so that as we are convinced of God's gentleness, we too will reflect such sweet care.

Gentle Entrance

Describing Christ again, the Greek word is used only once more in the gospels. Matthew 21 relates the account of Jesus' Triumphal Entry into Jerusalem to cheering crowds shouting, "Hosanna!" Later that same week, they would be crying for His crucifixion. Matthew quoted from the Old Testament when the prophet Zechariah predicted the manner in which the Messiah would come:

> Say to the daughter of Zion,
> "Behold your King is coming to you,
> Gentle, and mounted on a donkey,
> Even on a colt, the foal of a beast of burden." (Matt. 21:5)

While Christ will come in judgment and ruling power in His return, He first came to His people in humility, caring for their needs and paying for their sins. He allowed Himself to be crucified by the very people He created. He exerted the proper amount of force in His life on earth. Crucifixion did not happen by accident. He wasn't taken advantage of because He was too meek and mild. This was always God's plan, though definitely not the Jewish expectation.

Imagine the Jewish people in Galilee hearing Jesus enumerate the Beatitudes in the Sermon on the Mount. They would have been absolutely stunned by what He was teaching. Poorness of spirit was completely foreign to them. They were proud in spirit because they were Jews; they understood themselves already to be in the kingdom! In fact, everyone else must yield to them in order to gain entrance. The idea of mourning over their sin would have also been astonishing, since many, primarily the Pharisees, would have considered themselves righteous — they're God's people. They had the law. They didn't mourn over sin, but over the fact that all other nations weren't as godly as they were.

Consider the bewilderment on their faces as Christ revealed that the earth is conquered through gentleness. That was wholly contrary to their common understanding that conquering came through force. They were unwillingly subjugated by the Roman empire. They longed to cast off that yoke, and it was the Messiah who would lead the crusade to victory. The seeds of rejection in the crowd were already being scattered and sown in this introductory sermon of Jesus' earthly ministry. Undoubtedly, there were zealots in the audience who advocated and participated in armed resistance against the government.

The movement to revolt was coalescing during Christ's time, though it would not culminate until A.D. 70 when Emperor Titus wiped them out by the millions, essentially reducing Jerusalem and the temple to rubble. In the meantime, Jesus had gently arrived on the scene with the right amount of force in His first coming, submitting to both Roman and Jewish rulers, and yet triumphing. By gently coming underneath authorities who ranked infinitely beneath Him, He conquered sin, death, hell, and every earthly ruler.

But the Jewish mindset was radically different:

> You cannot win victories while mourning, and you certainly could never conquer Rome with meekness. In spite of all the miracles of His ministry, the people never really believed in Him as the Messiah, because He failed to act in military or miracle power against Rome.[4]

The oppressed desired to overtake their oppressors. The notion of "a meek Messiah leading meek people" was the polar opposite of their expectations.[5] The Jews recognized power and sought it. But Christ appeared with the bridled power of gentleness calling on all to come to Him in repentance and faith. This is the kind of power God desires for us to demonstrate as well.

Demonstrating Gentleness — Us

If we are to be faithful subjects of the kingdom and receive the blessing that God desires to bestow, how can we cultivate this biblical gentleness?

Humble Reception

We are in great need of the meekness that eagerly and humbly yields to the truth of God's Word. This begins with an internal attitude of the heart. James exhorted, "Therefore, putting aside all filthiness and all that remains of wickedness, *in humility receive the word implanted*, which is able to save your souls" (1:21, emphasis added). Embedding

---

4. MacArthur, *Matthew* (1985), 169.
5. MacArthur, *Matthew* (1985), 168.

the Word in our hearts is further explained in the prior verse that commands us to be "quick to hear, slow to speak and slow to anger" (v. 19). Our hearts must have a built-in readiness to heed God's Word and an ingrained reluctance to ever defy it. We forsake the forcefulness of heart that declares it will not be conquered by God—that unyieldingly seeks to exert its own will. Instead, by His grace, we humbly and happily subordinate our wills to the Lord as revealed in Scripture. Like grateful slaves, we gladly come underneath the will of our Master who sacrificed His very life for us.

Just as this volitional submission is necessary to enter the kingdom, it's also required to live within it. In fact, continued obedience confirms that entrance has truly been gained. *Believers are marked by our willingness to hear, understand, receive, and submit to God as His Spirit works in our hearts to make this subjection possible.* Prior to conversion, our defiant nature would have been neither able to submit to our Maker, nor even desire it. But when the Spirit regenerates man's wicked, corrupt heart, he no longer desires to bring glory to himself in everything he does. Before, he yearned for others to see his greatness and praise his accomplishments, but now in meekness, he longs for God to receive all glory, honor, and exaltation. God's will sets the agenda of his life.

When we imbibe God's Word, it assaults our sin and the remaining flesh within us. Believers engage in an inner battle. Paul explained, "For the flesh sets its desire against the Spirit, and the Spirit against the flesh; for these are in opposition to one another, so that you may not do the things that you please" (Gal. 5:17). Even as believers, we can cry in our hearts, *I will not yield! I know I'm supposed to obey, but I want my way!* We may struggle with submitting to the fallible authorities God has placed over us in the different spheres of our lives, but gentleness of heart concedes so that God's plans are accomplished.

Every biblical principle requires a gentle spirit in order to obey. We must conduct a search-and-destroy mission against any hardness of heart that would refuse to kneel. *Any area where we are not obeying God's Word is an area where we lack gentleness.* Perhaps you wrestle with honoring your strict, exasperating parents? Or respecting your sinful, selfish husband? Or praying for your abortion-promoting, government-bloating elected officials? Or loving the homosexual couple who live down the street? Or radically amputating that enslaving habit that dominates your life? Or sacrificially giving when finances are strained? Or joyfully surrendering your preferences in corporate worship? Or consistently disciplining your unwieldy, tiresome toddler? Or fully forgiving an offender who deeply betrayed your trust? Or working diligently for the lazy, vindictive manager? The list could go on and on. Where are we stubbornly refusing to yield to our gentle Lord? We must root it out to receive the blessing.

Sacrificial Service

We are not conquerors; we are servants. Christ didn't come so people would bow to us. Rather, we bend the knee before the Lord and call on others to do the same. During His ministry, James and John demanded that Christ seat them at His right hand when He reigns. The others were indignant only because the "Sons of Thunder" beat them to the punch, so Jesus addressed all of them:

> You know that those who are recognized as rulers of the Gentiles lord it over them; and their great men exercise authority over them. But it is not this way among you, but whoever wishes to become great among you shall be your servant; and whoever wishes to be first among you shall be slave of all. For even the Son of Man did not come to be served, but to serve, and to give His life a ransom for many. (Mark 10:42–45)

Christ contrasted kingdom living with worldly living. The difference is staggering. While those of the world coercively impose their will on others for personal gain, kingdom citizens seek their reward by quashing their own wills in order to serve others for Christ's sake. With such divergent means and ends, why would a believer ever operate in God's kingdom like a citizen of the world? Yet too often we do. We seek to carve out our own little territory. Our own family fought this battle continually at home when the children were younger. Everyone had their own little pieces of territory, whether it was in the room, on the bed, or in the car, and no one had better put their hands or stuff into that territory uninvited.

Sadly, as adults, we only become more adept at disguising our desires for our kingdoms and extending their boundaries by conquering more territories. Perhaps your home, and everything it encompasses, is your fortress. When someone crosses the line and disturbs your autonomy and peace, you react sinfully. We must instead imitate our Savior who came to sacrificially serve. We advance the Lord's kingdom by gaining ground through tender compassion and strength. Serving people is much more difficult than dominating them; it requires great power.

Reasonable Wisdom

In addressing godly wisdom, James inquired: "Who among you is wise and understanding? Let him show by his good behavior his deeds in the gentleness of wisdom" (3:13). There is a danger in wielding knowledge as a battering ram against others. Applying truth without discernment in relationships can hammer others into submission. Instead, gentle wisdom seeks to properly bring God's Word to bear in others' hearts and lives in such a way that they are strengthened, enabled, and encouraged to respond to it. James continued expounding on the nature of wisdom:

> But if you have bitter jealousy and selfish ambition
> in your heart, do not be arrogant and so lie against
> the truth. This wisdom is not that which comes

down from above, but is earthly, natural, demonic. For where jealousy and selfish ambition exist, there is disorder and every evil thing. But the wisdom from above is first pure, then peaceable, gentle, reasonable, full of mercy and good fruits, unwavering, without hypocrisy. And the seed whose fruit is righteousness is sown in peace by those who make peace. (3:14–18)

Gentleness thrives in the environment of humility, but it is squelched in the jealous, selfish, bitter, and ambitious heart. Always posturing and conniving, this heart clings to its own desires in order to exploit others. Gentle wisdom, however, has a ready willingness to be reasoned with, to stand corrected if necessary. Like love, it does not insist on its own way (1 Cor. 13:5). The reasonable spirit is always prepared to humbly yield to another's preferences and right judgments for the sake of furthering the kingdom and conforming to Christ.

Gracious Words

Kingdom citizens marked by humble sacrifice and reasonable wisdom will adorn their conduct with gracious speech. Like Christ, our words must use just the right amount of force needed, carefully considering the span of applicable biblical principles to bring the best possible result for others. To accomplish well, this presupposes "accurately handling the word of truth" (2 Tim. 2:15). Proverbs 15 states that a "gentle answer turns away wrath but a harsh word stirs up anger" (v. 1). When people sin against us, this doesn't mean we detach to avoid any possible conflict; rather, we engage with a carefully weighed and rightly motivated response. This gives them every opportunity to repent and respond rightly in the next exchange—this is loving gentleness. It dispenses "the truth in love" and offers up "only such a word as is good for edification according to the need of the moment, so that it will give grace to those who hear" (Eph. 4:15, 29).

Timing is another element of gracious words: "Like apples of gold in settings of silver is a word spoken in right circumstances" (Prov. 25:11). This grace-seasoned speech is wisely and thoughtfully considered and calibrated in every possible light to elicit God-pleasing responses (Col. 4:6). Clearly, it takes considerable effort and starts with a humble heart that seeks to know the truth and then lovingly and wisely apply it. The next verse in Proverbs 15 relates that the "tongue of the wise makes knowledge acceptable" (v. 2). These are words driven by a desire to see their hearer conformed to Christ's likeness. Much work in the kingdom of God is accomplished by our speech, so we must be pointedly mindful of it.

Tender Correction

How do we demonstrate gentleness when correcting and confronting others? It almost sounds like a contradiction in terms, but not when we remember what gentleness actually is. Christ's rebukes ranged from patiently reproving Thomas' doubt to zealously overturning the money changers' tables in the temple. He always used the perfect measure of righteously motivated force (John 20:27–29; 2:15). Learning the right amount of force not only depends on the circumstance, but also on the person in need of correction.

Gentle love takes a person's unique disposition into consideration; anyone with more than one child knows these distinctions well. For some children, it takes a single word of subdued reproof, and they wilt like a flower. Other children may ignore clear and direct chastisement altogether, oblivious that someone is even speaking to them. That response can still be gentle, but we must be careful that we're not actually excusing sinful anger. That said, using a quiet voice does not necessarily mean we have a properly controlled response either. I could have a muted volume and be out of control and devoid of gentleness. A hushed tone may be merely a means to getting what I want from my children rather than a longing for them to overcome their sin. So, the motivation that informs the correction matters.

It's the same within the church. Paul admonished, "Brethren, even if anyone is caught in any trespass, you who are spiritual, restore such a one in a spirit of gentleness; each one looking to yourself, so that you too will not be tempted" (Gal. 6:1–2). Believers are commanded to practice this tender correction with humility toward one another. Paul advised Timothy that the "Lord's bond-servant" must be "patient when wronged, with gentleness correcting those who are in opposition" (2 Tim. 2:24–25). As the Scripture gently admonishes us, so we correct others.

Considerate Evangelism

Our pleadings for others to respond to the cross must be characterized by gentleness. Peter encouraged believers to "always [be] ready to make a defense to everyone who asks you to give an account for the hope that is in you, *yet with gentleness and reverence*" (1 Pet. 3:15, emphasis added). Sadly, many have gone forth arrogantly proclaiming the gospel and mocking unbelievers in their wake. This derision can even be formalized and included in human origin debates and apologetics. Social media tends to fan these flames by providing relative anonymity and rewarding the digital tribalism whose prize of viral praise lies at the end of a tunnel so narrow that gentleness and respect are stripped entirely from the message.

Devoid of compassion, some harshly condemn unbelievers and taint their testimony with a harsh and embittered tone that undermines the great love that motivated Christ to accomplish our redemption in the first place. Instead, we must graciously and humbly present the truth with the meek and reverent spirit God requires. We bring the appropriate level of force to each situation, remembering that we too were once in blind ignorance and in bondage to sin: "Be peaceable, gentle, showing every consideration for all men for we also were once foolish ourselves" (Titus 3:2–3). Christ was forceful when needed, but never foolishly jesting or maliciously despising. Such behavior is worldly — why would our treatment of them match their own toward us? Why would we who have been freed from sin and indwelt with the Spirit present God's grace without grace? It should be the truth that offends and not our character, attitudes, or actions. We must heed the apostle's command to be meek and considerate as "ambassadors for Christ," begging on His behalf that others "be reconciled to God" (2 Cor. 5:20).

Patient Tolerance

We are also commanded to respond to the abrasiveness of others with gentle patience, particularly with one another in the church. Paul implored, "Walk in a manner worthy of the calling with which you have been called, with all humility and gentleness, with patience, showing tolerance for one another in love, being diligent to preserve the unity of the Spirit in the bond of peace" (Eph. 4:1–3). This kind of patience commits to bear with the sin that continues to emanate from other believers as we minister to them. This tolerant forbearance is absolutely critical in preserving unity within the church body. We must remain "knit[ted] together in love" (Col. 2:2), clinging to the oneness we all share in Christ in spite of the sinful flesh that remains in each of us. We forgive and bear with one another as we simultaneously bring God's Word to bear in each other's lives to look more like Christ.

Gentleness is fundamentally relational. We exercise it toward God and others. Many times, believers find it much easier to practice this submissive spirit before God than our fellow man. John Stott noted,

> I myself am quite happy to . . . call myself a "miserable sinner". It causes me no great problem. . . . But let somebody else come up to me after church and call me a miserable sinner, and I want to punch him on the nose! In other words, I am not prepared to allow

other people to think or speak of me what I have just acknowledged before God that I am.[6]

Meekness, he argued, fills in this hypocritical gap. Dr. David Martyn Lloyd-Jones echoed this observation:

> I am aware . . . of the sin and the evil that are within me, . . . but how much more difficult it is to allow other people to say things like that about me! I instinctively resent it. . . . I say of myself that I am a sinner, but instinctively I do not like anybody else to say I am a sinner.[7]

As we grow in meekness, the ability to receive our true estimation from others will also grow. As we are saturated in the truths of Scripture, we will believe and embrace to a greater degree who we truly are on our own and in Christ.

Caring Leadership

Gentleness is required as a qualification for church leadership. Mentioned in 1 Timothy, Paul distinguished an elder as one who is "not addicted to wine or pugnacious, but gentle, peaceable, free from the love of money" (3:3). Instead of a combative, contentious nature, shepherds must deal gently with their flocks—firm when necessary, but never as harsh taskmasters using disproportionate force or "lording it over those allotted to [their] charge" (1 Pet. 5:3). This gentleness is driven by a deep consideration for the congregation. Paul exemplified such a manner toward the church at Thessalonica:

---

6. John R. W. Stott, *The Message of the Sermon on the Mount*, rev. ed. (Downers Grove: Intervarsity Press, 2020), 26.
7. D. Martyn Lloyd-Jones, *Studies in the Sermon on the Mount* (Grand Rapids: Eerdmans, 2000), 54.

> But we proved to be gentle among you, as a nursing mother tenderly cares for her own children. Having so fond an affection for you, we were well-pleased to impart to you not only the gospel of God but also our own lives, because you had become very dear to us. (1 Thess. 2:7–8)

It's a travesty that many within the church have been deeply hurt by church leaders who abused their power. Well-known names have dotted national headlines as their ministry empires have been exposed to be driven by anger, dominance, and manipulation. But there are even more pastoral tyrants lacking the status of celebrity who commit the exploitation and abuse among their flocks. Informed by Paul's heartfelt concern, church leadership must maintain a similar spirit when accomplishing the necessary work of confronting, reproving, exhorting, admonishing, disciplining, and leading.

The Reward

Christ promised that kingdom citizens who exercise gentleness will be rewarded with inheriting the earth. What does that mean? We tend to think that if we don't elbow, jockey, shove, and wrangle for our own interests, we will be left deprived. We will have nothing. But Christ said unless we are gentle, we will receive nothing. Unless we lay aside our own sinfully immoderate force to meet our own desires, we will gain nothing. We don't have to desperately grasp at everything in this life since Christ has made eternal provision for us.

With this truth, Peter comforted those who were being persecuted. As they were clinging to Christ over the things of this world, the apostle reminded them of the forthcoming blessing, "an inheritance which is imperishable and undefiled and will not fade away, reserved in heaven" (1 Pet. 1:4). The term *inheritance* is most often mentioned in

Scripture to describe the benefit of salvation and the eternal life it provides. Christ used the future tense in this Beatitude, so He was eyeing His return to establish His millennial kingdom here on earth before giving way to the eternal state. We will rule and reign with Him, but in this life, God calls us to faithfully yield our wills in humble meekness. Christ later pronounced:

> And everyone who has left houses or brothers or sisters or father or mother or children or farms for My name's sake, will receive many times as much, and will inherit eternal life. But many who are first will be last; and the last, first. (Matt. 19:29–30)

We get it all when we give it all up: our wills, desires, pleasures, achievements, and all the coercive posturing and deceitful tactics required to gain them. If we are willing to forfeit everything in gentleness, we will be rewarded with far superior blessings in return.

~

Blest are the meek, who stand afar
from rage and passion, noise and war;
God will secure their happy state,
and plead their cause against the great.

~Isaac Watts, 1709

Questions for Reflection & Discussion

1. Before reading this chapter, how did you define gentleness?

2. After having read this chapter, define the biblical understanding of gentleness.

3. Describe how God demonstrates His attribute of gentleness. Give some scriptural examples. Why is it important to understand God's gentleness before exercising our own?

4. Describe examples of Christ's gentleness.

5. Submission is a key component of gentleness. Review the list of questions on page 91. Are any of these struggles for you? If so, what truths has God given to enable you to demonstrate humble submission in these areas?

6. How easy are you to be reasoned with? Are you servant-minded toward others, not insisting on your own way? If not, what is one action you can prayerfully take today? Tomorrow? And the day after?

7. How well is your speech (the content, tone, and timing) seeking to help others look more like Christ? Seek to memorize Ephesians 4:29 this month and find opportunities to put off (what not to say) and put on (what to say).

8. Are you involved enough in your church body to have ample opportunities to exercise patience and tolerance? If not, why not?

9. Like Stott and Lloyd-Jones, do you find it difficult to be confronted by others? Look up the following references and identify sins that may underlie our resistance to correction: Isa. 30:9-10; Matt. 23:5-7; John 12:42-43; Phil. 2:3.

10. What does it mean to "inherit the earth"?

11. Examine your life: Are there any areas where you have not yet fully yielded? Are there any idols in your life which you are hopelessly clutching? For believers, the gospel enables us to release our grip. Consider any areas of life where you have not humbly yielded to God and neighbor. Cry out to the Lord to build a humble, gentle heart within you, so that you become a more useful and pleasing citizen of the kingdom.

Chapter 5

Blessed Are Those Who Hunger and Thirst for Righteousness

Blessed are those who hunger and thirst for righteousness,
for they shall be satisfied.

America's Declaration of Independence famously affirms, "We hold these truths to be self-evident, that all men are created equal, that they are endowed by their Creator with certain unalienable Rights, that among these are Life, Liberty and the pursuit of Happiness."[1] Excluding God's Abrahamic Covenant to create a chosen nation, the declaration was arguably the greatest statement ever penned at a nation's founding. It purposely adds no limitations to the idea of "happiness," and yet this lack of qualification has led to conflicting explanations and disastrous consequences.[2]

---

1. Thomas Jefferson, "The Declaration of Independence," https://www.archives.gov/founding-docs/declaration-transcript.
2. John MacArthur, *Matthew 1–7*, vol. 1, *The MacArthur New Testament Commentary* (Chicago: Moody Press, 1985), 178.

Left to the depraved hearts of men, their own pursuits of personal happiness will always be warped and wanting. They can never be truly fulfilled. Thankfully, as citizens of a superior kingdom, we have a far better manifesto—a truly divine document that explains the meaning of happiness, reveals the manner by which it is achieved, and promises its fulfillment.

Christ shared the Beatitudes so that we can learn about these various aspects of joyful kingdom living. We have studied the first three blessings and are once again surprised. True satisfaction in life comes through the unlikely source of self-denying holiness. This is not the Pharisees' self-righteousness, but a true goodness that is both defined and granted by God. America's Founders were wise to never guarantee happiness, only the pursuit of it. But Jesus could faithfully promise that the pursuit of holiness would always bring true happiness. *An essential component of the kingdom of God, true righteousness, therefore, is guaranteed to those who passionately seek for it.*

We've already discovered that the character qualities listed in the Beatitudes are necessary to gain entrance into the kingdom through salvation. That is, the Holy Spirit's initial work in the heart produces the beginning of these attitudes which prompt us to turn to Christ in repentance and faith. Then, the Spirit nurtures these attitudes to enable us to live as devout kingdom citizens. For example, we cannot enter until we recognize our spiritual bankruptcy. As we grow in humility in our Christian walk, we will ever increasingly be reminded of our own impoverished state compared to the glories and goodness of God. Our gratitude will multiply accordingly as we better grasp the immensity of His provision in giving His Word, His Spirit, and access to His kingdom.

With the blessings of poverty, grief, and meekness burning away the vestiges of arrogance in our hearts, a growing, insatiable desire for true righteousness emerges. Any areas in our lives where we are unhappy and dissatisfied are areas where we lack holiness.

Holiness solves everything. It's the very nature of God. Christ promised that those who seek after righteousness will be fully satisfied, so we should pursue this holiness with reckless abandon.

Defining Hunger, Thirst, & Righteousness

Since Christ employed metaphors in this blessing, we must carefully understand His meaning. When He spoke of hunger and thirst, He wasn't referring to food and drink. Rather, He alluded to the underlying desire for fulfillment. To hunger is simply to have the need to eat — more broadly, to have the longing to fill that which is empty; namely, our stomachs. Teenage boys might understand this better than anyone. Hunger seems to be their constant companion. When my son was younger, he would wander through the kitchen and entire food products would suddenly disappear. It seemed he had a bottomless pit for a stomach.

Thirst is, just as simply, the need to drink — to have dryness and an accompanying desire to have that parched palate quenched. While humans can live without food for an extended period of time, we can only live a short time without water to slake our thirst.

When living in California, we took a few excursions into the plains and deserts below the mountains. In a place like Death Valley, one experiences this thirst very quickly if an insufficient amount of water has been packed. The growing urge to rehydrate the body with fluids rapidly escalates. The mouth dries, and the tongue sticks to the roof of the mouth as the lips blister and chap from the arid climate. Christ used these visceral, relatable metaphors purposely to strike at the very core of who we are. Essentially, we could have everything else in life, but if we don't have food and water, we will perish.

Likewise, Christ is pointing out man's need for spiritual sustenance. Even more critical than physical provision is our need for spiritual righteousness, but man's corrupt, sinful heart cannot even discern this need. When men and women are awakened to this need at salvation, their appetites for holiness begin and continue to grow sharper. Because believers are grateful recipients of God's kind, unmerited favor, they will desperately yearn for this righteousness.

Those who are blessed, then, are those who perceive their desperate need to be filled in the area of holiness. Righteousness is neither humanly defined nor is it simply morality; rather, *righteousness is that which conforms to the law of God.* Essentially, God's law is an expression of His very nature. Thus, to be perfectly righteous would be to perfectly conform to His character. Apart from Christianity, the world grossly misdefines righteousness, mischaracterizing it as a subjective code of self-defined ethics or merely performing some well-intentioned good deeds. Within the metaphor, Christ communicated that man's need for righteousness is essential to life, so let's carefully define it next.

First, we must recognize God's perfect standard. Until we know that exists, we can't desire it. We don't come into the world crying out of an innate awareness of our need for holiness. We clamor for physical nourishment. Without it, we die. Sadly, many who've suffered the horrifying pangs of starvation vividly remember how food dominated their every waking moment. However, apart from God opening our eyes, we are entirely blind to our great need for righteousness. Because of our sinful nature, humanity is spiritually "dead in . . . trespasses and sins" (Eph. 2:1). In fact, we desire the opposite. In wicked lawlessness, we rebelliously oppose the very thing we need.

Next, once we recognize that God's standard of righteousness is moral perfection, we need to realize that we have failed to meet that standard. We are consummately disqualified as we are comprehensively corrupt. In speaking to the pagan Athenians on the Acropolis, Paul declared that God "has fixed a day in which He will judge the world in righteousness through a Man whom He has appointed, having furnished proof to all men by raising Him from the dead" (Acts 17:31–32). God will judge us according to that perfect standard — His righteousness, not ours. It's His definition, His character, His standard, and His judgment. We don't get to choose our own standards and make the self-determination that we are righteous.

The Athenians should have openly repented and confessed that they had fallen short of God's true, objective, and authoritative standard. Confession entails acknowledging God's assessment of our condition in light of Himself, including the judgment. We agree with God that we deserve eternal condemnation for impugning His holy character. Because He is infinitely holy, a lawbreaker could never satisfy the penalty. In Psalm 32, David agreed:

> I acknowledged my sin to You,
> And my iniquity I did not hide;
> I said, "I will confess my transgressions to the Lord";
> And You forgave the guilt of my sin. (v. 5)

We all have a natural propensity to conceal and thereby deny our sin. We refuse to be convinced of the weightiness of our wrongdoing. We minimize it, rationalize it, and then tuck it away in our minds, so that the conscience is muffled or even seared. Instead, we must rightly and openly admit falling short of God's holy requirements. We covered much of this in chapter 3 when David demonstrated how to properly mourn over sin. Revisiting Psalm 51, we glimpse inside David's heart:

> Wash me thoroughly from my iniquity
> And cleanse me from my sin.
> For I know my transgressions,
> And my sin is ever before me.
> Against You, You only, I have sinned
> And done what is evil in Your sight,
> So that You are justified when You speak
> And blameless when You judge.
> Behold, I was brought forth in iniquity,

And in sin my mother conceived me. (vv. 2–5)

God has clearly communicated in His Word that "all have sinned and fall short of the glory of God" (Rom. 3:23). We will never hunger and thirst for righteousness until we first agree with God that we are devoid of any. Many believe they may partner with Christ by partaking of His righteousness and contributing some of their own. They refuse to relinquish the idea that there is some kernel of inner goodness with which they can commend themselves to God. To devastate their pride and admit the ugly truth is simply a line they cannot cross. Their instinctive sense of self-love and self-rightness is insurmountable: "Every man's way is right in his own eyes" (Prov. 21:2).

The Bible uses the metaphor of hunger and thirst in another passage. Scripture defines our sinful erring as an attempt to slake our hunger and thirst with anything other than God. This amounts to idolatry. God related to the prophet Jeremiah:

> For My people have committed two evils:
> They have forsaken Me,
> The fountain of living waters,
> To hew for themselves cisterns,
> Broken cisterns
> That can hold no water. (Jer. 2:13)

God described rebellion against Him as rejecting the very One who can satisfy all needs. Portraying Himself as the "fountain of living waters," God implied not only that true fulfillment is found solely in Him, but that any replacement will invariably be ultimately unsatisfying. The facade of gratification is as fleeting as water in a leaky bucket. Carving out a space for idols in our hearts mocks God's provision of righteousness as insufficient. He rightly condemns as wicked both the forsaking and replacing of Himself by men.

By contrast, those who hunger and thirst for righteousness long to think and live according to God's holy character revealed by Christ and His Word. Once we recognize our need, we must possess the desire to have that need met. We neither wallow hopelessly in our own inadequacies nor try even harder to manufacture self-righteousness. We must acquire the taste for God's righteousness. Just as men have an innate desire to eat and even find enjoyment in food and drink, so too the believer has a yearning for righteousness and rejoices in it.

However, Christians can become like a cancer patient in the thick of chemotherapy. The strong treatment suppresses the appetite. In fact, patients must actively ensure proper nourishment is not neglected, since their internal alarm for sustenance has been overwhelmed by the powerful drugs. In the same way, the sickness of sin can override our desire for holiness. We can revert to behavior that characterized our unbelieving state. Like the world, we can desire happiness and not necessarily holiness. But we must remember: *In order to be happy, we must be holy.*

Imagine a man crossing the vast, sunbaked Sahara. He feebly summits sand dune after sand dune only to survey the vast expanse of barren wasteland still before him. His eyes ache to rest on any shade of green, hoping to spy a lush oasis that could offer refreshment from his weary journey. What if we came and offered him a new set of clothes to replace his dusty, tattered outfit? Or told him about a new show to binge watch as a distraction from his trial? His bewildered expression would sufficiently communicate his thought—*You are insane! I need water!* All his waking thoughts and actions are driven by this single desire. Are we this desperate when it comes to righteousness? What are we wasting our time with instead? What other cravings crowd out our hunger for holiness? *The more we grow in our understanding of who God is, the more we will be satisfied with nothing else.*

In this sermon containing the Beatitudes, Jesus was addressing a large crowd that included many who sought physical provision from Him. Yet He was preaching about their spiritual need. Later in the sermon, Christ commanded, "But seek first His kingdom and His righteousness, and all these things will be added to you" (Matt. 6:33). God will faithfully care for the physical needs of His kingdom citizens while we pursue the work He has purposed for us to complete. In fact, the pursuit of righteousness tends to remove our desires for its substitutes.

When Israel pursued other gods in the Old Testament, God questioned them: "Why do you spend money for what is not bread, and your wages for what does not satisfy?" (Isa. 55:2). He pointed out the futility of their efforts. Envision our desert wanderer finally happening upon a village and with the remaining handful of coins in his threadbare pocket, purchasing fake, decorative fruit on display. The sheen on the plastic makes it appear ripe and enticing, but what's going to happen when he takes that first bite? Not satisfaction.

When my three girls were younger, I found food all over my house, but it wasn't edible. They enjoyed their little kitchen and culinary toys, but we couldn't eat that food. What foolishness for our desert friend to imagine anything life-giving would be found in that pretend fruit just because of its appearance, but that's how unbelievers live their lives.

Sadly, believers can also behave in this way even though we know better. We pursue things that cannot satisfy. Students may seek academic accolades. Lonely singles may seek a relationship. Careerists may seek worldly success. The weekend warrior may seek adventure. The soon-to-be retiree may seek financial security. The awkward teenager may seek social acceptance. The tired mom may seek peace and quiet. The disgruntled employee may seek ease and distraction. But apart from God and His righteousness, we're expending time, energy, and resources on plastic fruit.

Instead, God tenderly appealed to Israel:

> Ho! Every one who thirsts, come to the waters;
> And you who have no money come, buy and eat.

Come, buy wine and milk
Without money and without cost . . .
Listen carefully to Me, and eat what is good,
And delight yourself in abundance. (55:1–2)

God's call to hunger and thirst for righteousness isn't a legalistic life that constantly bears the heavy load of external religious law-keeping. It's a pursuit that brings joy, satisfaction, and freedom, but it will elude those who simultaneously try to have their needs met by the world. It is a passionate and continual pursuit of Christ through the Word of God as our only true source of fulfillment. John MacArthur puts it this way:

> Jesus declares that the deepest desire of every person ought to be to hunger and thirst for righteousness. That is the Spirit-prompted desire that will lead a person to salvation and keep him strong and faithful once he is in the kingdom. It is also the only ambition that, when fulfilled, brings enduring happiness.[3]

This pursuit, then, is a fundamental aspect of kingdom living for the believer, but why?

The Need for Righteousness

Why is being clothed with Christ's righteousness necessary to enter the kingdom and live within it? To receive God's favor, we *must* be declared holy. Many modern gospel presentations today proclaim that people are in need of love, and God can fill that need. While true, God has already demonstrated and extended that love in the person and work of Jesus Christ. Our evangelistic appeals must first be root-

---

3. MacArthur, *Matthew* (1985), 178.

ed in a need for a righteousness we do not possess. We do not need God to fill a love-starved, God-shaped vacuum in our hearts; we need Him to fill our sinful, human-shaped depravity of heart with a true righteousness that allows us to be reconciled to Him. God imparting His righteousness to us *is* His expression of love and the means by which we experience the fullness of it:

> Hunger and thirst represent the necessities of physical life. Jesus' analogy demonstrates that righteousness is required for spiritual life just as food and water are required for physical life. Righteousness is not an optional spiritual supplement but a spiritual necessity. We can no more live spiritually without righteousness than we can live physically without food and water.[4]

Perceived through the lens of justification and sanctification, there are two distinct categories of righteousness. Justification is required for admission into the kingdom, while sanctification is reserved for living within it. Though this beatitude refers to the second, it is highly imperative the two are not confused, so let's address both in detail.

Righteousness for Kingdom Entrance

On the heels of the Beatitudes, Jesus preached that "unless [our] righteousness surpasses that of the scribes and Pharisees, [we] will not enter the kingdom of heaven" (Matt. 5:20). There is a righteousness required to gain admittance, but it eclipses a mere pharisaical, external conformity to the law. The required standard is God's own holiness. Christ revealed the criterion for admission, summing up: "You are to be perfect, as your heavenly Father is perfect" (5:48). Judged by this standard, we

---

4. MacArthur, *Matthew* (1985), 178.

have earned a guilty verdict. We are in great need of the righteousness of justification—Christ's perfect righteousness. It is entirely outside of ourselves. We cannot earn it, produce it, or exercise it. His own righteousness must be imputed, or assigned, to us based on His sacrifice. Paul, as every believer must, experienced this personally. He recounted to the Philippians his own seemingly righteous pedigree. If anyone could reach the level of holiness required, Paul would have been the perfect candidate:

> Circumcised the eighth day, of the nation of Israel, of the tribe of Benjamin, a Hebrew of Hebrews; as to the Law, a Pharisee; as to zeal, a persecutor of the church; as to the righteousness which is in the Law, found blameless. (Phil. 3:5–6)

He wasn't actually perfect, but as a self-righteous Pharisee, he meticulously kept external rules, which included proper temple sacrifice to cover sin. But as Charles Spurgeon preached, "The greatest enemy to human souls . . . is the self-righteous spirit which makes men look to themselves for salvation."[5]

Not only was this self-righteousness insufficient, but Paul later considered those attempts worthless and condemnatory rather than meritorious. After receiving Christ's righteousness instead, Paul knew he didn't have "a righteousness of [his] own derived from the Law, but that which is through faith in Christ, the righteousness which comes from God on the basis of faith" (3:9). The Father ordained "Him who knew no sin to be sin on our behalf, so that we might become the righteousness of God in Him" (2 Cor. 5:21). *Jesus' perfect righteousness is the only ticket into the kingdom, and it can be accredited to us by God on the basis of faith.*

---

5. Charles H. Spurgeon, "Soul Satisfaction," *The Complete Works of Charles Spurgeon,* vol. 55, sermon no. 3137, delivered at Metropolitan Tabernacle, transcript published in Newington, 1909, https://www.ccel.org/ccel/spurgeon/sermons 55.xiii.html.

While on the cross, Christ absorbed the wrath we justly accrued from rebelling against our Creator. Through our myriad infractions against His perfect character as manifested in His law, we violated His holiness from our depraved condition. When He willingly took the penalty upon Himself, God's holy wrath was satisfied. Those who repent and trust in Christ's redeeming work have their legal status before God changed. While Christ received *our* just punishment, we receive credit for *His* life of perfect obedience to the Father. What an exchange! Instead of being found guilty as unclean lawbreakers whose "righteous deeds are like a filthy garment" (Isa. 64:6), we are now no longer under condemnation (Rom. 8:1). We are declared legally justified; the debt has been fully paid (Col. 2:14). Further, we have been clothed in Christ's perfect righteousness granted to us by grace through faith with no merit of our own—in fact "while we were yet sinners, Christ died for us" (Rom. 5:8).

Paul broke it down in Romans 3, clearly establishing that all men are judged by God's law, which is the standard of perfection. He proclaimed that "all have sinned and fall short of the glory of God" (v. 23). For those who turn to Christ, they are "justified as a gift by His grace through the redemption which is in Christ Jesus; whom God displayed publicly as a propitiation in His blood through faith" (vv. 24–25). God's righteousness was demonstrated not only by Christ's life—through His innate character and His ministry and obedience on earth—but through His death as well, as the Father's just wrath was appeased in His Son's sacrifice on our behalf. The cross, Paul concluded, demonstrated God as both "just and the justifier of the one who has faith in Jesus" (v. 26).

We must possess a perfect, infinite righteousness in order to secure an eternal relationship with the infinitely holy Sovereign of the universe. Scripture couldn't be clearer that our own morality and good works can *never* accomplish this, nor even contribute to it. It is entirely God's special and undeserved gift on the sole basis of Christ's work. Referencing Adam, the first man and representative of the sinful human race, and Christ as the second Adam, Paul argued:

> For if by the transgression of the one (Adam), death reigned through the one, much more those who receive the abundance of grace and of the gift of righteousness will reign in life through the One, Jesus Christ. So then as through one transgression there resulted condemnation to all men, even so through one act of righteousness there resulted justification of life to all men. For as through the one man's disobedience the many were made sinners, even so through the obedience of the One the many will be made righteous. (Rom. 5:17–19, parentheses added)

This type of righteousness, called justification or *judicial holiness*, is unilaterally accorded to us. It is fully sufficient; it never changes or grows. It doesn't need to because it's Christ's perfect righteousness. The recipients of this beatitude who hunger and thirst, however, refer to the second category of righteousness.

Righteousness for Kingdom Living

Through our regeneration, we have been brought from spiritual death to spiritual life (Eph. 2:5). Believers are indwelt by the Holy Spirit and are made new creatures (2 Cor. 5:17). Thus, once we are brought into the kingdom by Christ's sacrificial work, we are enabled to live within His realm in a manner that accomplishes actual righteous behavior. This other kind of righteousness, sometimes referred to as *practical holiness* or *personal holiness*, pertains to our sanctification. This righteousness is produced in cooperation with the Spirit who empowers us by the truth of the Word to grow in conformity to Christ's character. He works within us and through us, "instructing us to deny ungodliness and worldly desires and to live sensibly, righteously and godly in the present age" (Titus 2:11), all while we pursue Him with our renewed mind, will, and affections. By God's grace, we increasingly become what we have been called to be—holy. This holiness is manifested in righteous acts that progressively reflect God's own nature as He shapes us into "the measure of the stature which belongs to the fullness of Christ" (Eph. 4:13). We must never confuse or conflate these two types of righteousness. Whereas justification is a onetime declaration performed entirely by the completed work of Christ, sanctification is an actual transformation that involves our inner man's participation and develops over time.

When we perform the "good works, which God prepared beforehand so we would walk in them" (Eph. 2:10), they in no way increase our justification or add to Christ's saving work on our behalf. When God gives new hearts to unbelievers, He places His "Spirit within [them] and causes [them] to walk in [His] statutes, and [they] will be careful to observe [His] ordinances" (Ezek. 36:27). Kingdom citizens have been given new desires that will always flow outward in a love and longing for the holiness empowered by the indwelling Spirit. With this new heart and the Spirit's power through the Word, believers put to death the fleshly sin that remains and train themselves through the spiritual disciplines to pursue God's commands. This is how John the Baptist could issue forth a call to "bear fruit in keeping with repentance" (Matt. 3:8). Peter exhorted,

> As obedient children, do not be conformed to the former lusts which were yours in your ignorance, but like the Holy One who called you, be holy yourselves also in all your behavior; because it is written, "You shall be holy, for I am holy." (1 Pet. 1:14–16)

At salvation, we are placed in union with Christ, and through sanctification our hearts continually yearn to look like our Savior. Hunger and thirst for righteousness result from these deeply implanted desires. In fact, if upon close self-examination, you find them entirely absent, it's possible you may not have truly partaken of the righteousness Christ imputes to believers' accounts. Speaking of Christ's promised return for His church, the apostle John confirmed that "everyone who has this hope fixed on Him purifies himself, just as He is pure" (1 John 3:3). Do you long for Christ's return? Is the trajectory of your life, including your priorities, reflective of that hope?

While justification and sanctification are separate, they always go hand in hand. It is helpful to look for indications of the latter to ensure the former has taken place. Christ warned of false converts throughout His entire ministry. If evidence of sanctification is nonexistent, you must return to the truths of the gospel and cry out to God for a poorness of spirit and true mourning over your sin. For believers, their motivations are now properly directed. Far from the felt needs that many in Jesus' audience desired to be met, kingdom citizens know that "the kingdom of God is not eating and drinking, but righteousness and peace and joy in the Holy Spirit" (Rom. 14:17). Sometimes the evidence is sparse, but it is still there. A. W. Tozer observed:

> Hunger is . . . God's merciful provision, a divinely sent stimulus to propel us in the direction of food. . . . [Thirst] is nature's last drastic effort to rouse the imperiled life to seek to renew itself. A dead body feels no hunger and the dead soul knows not the pangs of holy desire. . . . Our desire for fuller life is proof that some life must be there already. Our very dissatisfactions should encourage us, our yet unfulfilled aspirations should give us hope.[6]

---

6. A.W. Tozer, *The Size of the Soul: Principles of Revival and Spiritual Growth*, (Chicago: Moody, 1993), 12.

We still sin and ongoing repentance is still necessary, but our primary and defining passions are Christ and Christlikeness.

Acquiring an Appetite for Righteousness

If sanctification requires our participation, how can we hone our appetites for righteousness? How do we practice hungering and thirsting for holiness? Physical hunger and thirst require no such training, but because our sinfulness blunts our appetites, we must whet them. As believers mature toward Christlikeness, their hunger and thirst for holiness will actually sharpen.

When we adopted our two youngest girls from Haiti, my wife and I had determined that we were optimally situated—right at the point of having sufficient physical energy to undertake the challenge, but also enough experience in parenting to hopefully rise to the occasion. We were wrong on both counts. We didn't have enough energy, and we fell flat on our faces. We quickly discovered that as prepared as we thought we were, we weren't. It should have been evident all along, however, because even though we improved in our abilities to parent, we were able to better discern our lack of righteousness in that area of our lives. By God's grace, He used that resulting humility to grow us into His Son's image as we depended on Him for everything. Let's consider some ways to grow our appetites for righteousness.

Cultivate a Passion for God

While this desire is fundamental to Christians, it must still be wrought within us. Because of our sin, it doesn't spring forth without careful cultivation. Faithful citizens must study, meditate on, understand, appreciate, and rehearse the person and work of Christ in their souls. Then we apply those truths in specific ways to our daily lives so as to reflect Him and accomplish His work. The psalmist likened our desire for God to a deer for water:

As the deer pants for the water brooks,
So my soul pants for You, O God.
My soul thirsts for God, for the living God;
When shall I come and appear before God? (Ps. 42:1–2)

The illustration is not of a gentle doe gracefully lapping a sip of cool water in an idyllic landscape depicting tranquility. Rather, the imagery portrays a desperate deer being hunted to the point of exhaustion and in need of the reviving sustenance water provides; otherwise, the stalked prey will be overtaken. That's how our souls should pant for God, longing to be in His presence. David cried out,

O God, You are my God; I shall seek You earnestly;
My soul thirsts for You, my flesh yearns for You,
In a dry and weary land where there is no water. (Ps. 63:1)

David expressed the emptiness that the world offers. Rightness and goodness cannot be found in this world, but in God alone. Scripture aptly links this metaphor of hunger and thirst with the pursuit of God.

If, upon self-reflection, this passion for Him is absent within professing believers upon, then either they do not truly know God, or they've never been taught to develop this yearning. The Holy Spirit who indwells true believers is passionate for the Father and His Son; some measure of this will always be present. But it may simply be that some believers are ignorant of their Savior's character. Thankfully, the more we learn about who God is, our hunger and thirst will be subsequently amplified. Thus, we wholeheartedly seek Him through continual immersion in His Word. A sermon on Sunday is insufficient. We cannot pant after God once a week for a few hours. It is an ongoing quest to know Him and what He desires from us.

This pursuit extends into heaven. Imagine having no sin to curb our appetites for God—nothing that will keep us from Him. All of eternity will simultaneously be a constant fulfillment that never ends. There's no point of satiety. The hunger and thirst will always be present, but always totally filled. We will never be able to get enough of God and yet be so perfectly satisfied.[7] Nothing in the world comes close to such a feast.

Fix Your Eyes on Jesus

The author of Hebrews exhorted his audience to fix their "eyes on Jesus, the author and perfecter of faith" (12:2). Commonly misused, this phrase is not some mystical exercise, nor some empty cliché devoid of meaning. *It is considering and being convinced of the objective realities about Christ's person and work which lead to an experiential joy in Christ's presence that is grounded in biblical truth.* The two always go together. Christ declared, "I am the bread of life; he who comes to Me will not hunger, and he who believes in Me will never thirst" (John 6:35). He is the life-giving bread who satisfies the hunger of our souls. He offers Himself to a world in desperate need of Him. Earlier in His ministry, Christ professed to the woman at the well, "Whoever drinks of the water that I will give him shall never thirst; but the water that I will give him will become in him a well of water springing up to eternal life" (John 4:14). This water is the Spirit of God, washing and cleansing the soul from sin and implanting the desire and resources for holiness.

Christ declared in John's vision: "I am the Alpha and the Omega, the beginning and the end. I will give to the one who thirsts from the spring of the water of life without cost" (Rev. 21:6). While longingly anticipating the Savior's return, John concluded, "Let the one who is thirsty come; let the one who wishes take the water of life without cost" (22:17). When salvation is taken hold of, the believer continually partakes from the fountain of holiness that is Christ. Fixing our gaze upon Him both increases and satisfies our desire for Him.

7. MacArthur, *Matthew* (1985), 183-184.

Fellowship with God's People

Next, we must be with the people of God. With Christ ascended and the church established, it is now through His bride that we witness God's righteousness demonstrated in practical ways. We see Scripture's truth lived out among believers as they function together as members of a localized body. God designed this community of the redeemed to help each individual "grow up in all aspects into Him who is the head, even Christ, from whom the whole body, being fitted and held together by what every joint supplies, according to the proper working of each individual part, causes the growth of the body for the building up of itself in love" (Eph. 4:15–16).

Neglecting God's people, then, necessarily devastates our spiritual appetites for holiness. In its place will grow a hardness of heart. Hebrews admonishes:

> Take care, brethren, that there not be in any one of you an evil, unbelieving heart that falls away from the living God. But encourage one another day after day, as long as it is still called "Today," so that none of you will be hardened by the deceitfulness of sin. (3:12–13)

My wife and I had the privilege of spending our twenty-fifth wedding anniversary in Hawaii. While it was such a joyful time together alone, we understood that the very state of our precious marriage would be upended if severed from the local church. It would quickly descend into a sinful disregard of God and His will. Sadly, the thousands of honeymooners and anniversary celebrators on the islands were chasing a relational happiness that only God and His family can bring. Even believers who forsake the assembling together will soon find themselves inured to sin's deception. Our sanctification occurs in a communal context as we are "living stones . . . being built up as a spiritual house for a holy priesthood" (1 Pet. 2:5). We see

Christ and His holiness through His church living out His commands by the Spirit's power.

Flee from Sin

As we endeavor to seek after righteousness, we must hate anything that keeps us from that which satisfies our hunger and thirst. Sin warps our palettes so as to crave after worldly lusts, but we must flee from sin with the greatest urgency. On that Hawaiian trip, we hiked up a dormant volcano. Its last eruption dated back to 1790, so we were feeling quite safe. But had it erupted at that moment with the blistering lava blazing toward us, what should have been our response? "Run!" It would never be: "Ooh, that's mesmerizing. Let's touch it to see what it feels like. Better yet, why not dive in? A lava bath sounds delightful!" No, we would flee for our lives.

That's how we should treat sin. It should be like scorching lava to us because it threatens to consume us. It contorts and redirects us from the holiness we desire. If sin provides pleasure and joy in our lives, then we will hunger and thirst after it. We cannot have an appetite for both wickedness and righteousness at the same time. With God's strength, we must run from fleshly desires while He is burning them away and replacing them with a love for righteousness. Paul admonished Timothy to "flee from these things, you man of God, and pursue righteousness, godliness, faith, love, perseverance and gentleness" (1 Tim. 6:11).

Meditate on the Word of God

God's Word contains "everything pertaining to life and godliness" (2 Pet. 1:3), including God's attributes and the principles that enable us to reflect His character. Transformative change resides in the power of God's revelation; as such, believers must saturate themselves in biblical truth. Psalm 119 is clear: "How can a young man keep his way pure? By keeping it according to Your word" (v. 9). It's one of the most basic verses in the entire Bible, but are we doing it? Are we consistently digging in the Word to gain wisdom and know what pleases Him? If we desire to be righteous, we must meditate on the Word. Like the psalmist, can we affirm, "Your word I have treasured in my heart, that I may not sin against You" (v. 11)? How much quality time do we devote to cherishing God's Word, mulling it over, considering it, studying it, pondering it, memorizing it, and marinating in it? *To the extent we immerse ourselves in His Word we will love righteousness.*

Like sin, neglecting the Word blunts the appetite for holiness; and like prayer, when we forget our state of dependence, we fail to see our desperate need for His life-giving words. We must "like newborn babies, long for the pure milk of the word, so that by it [we] may grow in respect to salvation" (1 Pet. 2:2). Do we remember that "all Scripture is inspired by God and profitable for teaching, for reproof, for correction, for training in righteousness" (2 Tim. 3:16)? We must wisely appropriate those principles and apply them to our daily lives—to both moral circumstances and the humdrum of mundane activities. We must think about politics righteously and create our to-do lists righteously; discipline our child righteously and change a diaper righteously; relate to our spouses righteously and spend and save righteously; interact with coworkers righteously and manage our smartphones righteously. *Everything we need to both cultivate and slake our desire for righteousness is found in the pages of Scripture as illuminated by the Holy Spirit.*

Obey the Word of God

Many reading this book may regularly pursue the spiritual disciplines. Some may blast expository preaching in their earbuds around the clock, but there may be a growing divide between their formal and functional theology. We love truth, but *are we obeying it?* How do we fare at practically living out truth? The apostle John doesn't mince words when he pronounced, "The one who practices righteousness is righteous, just as He is righteous" (1 John 3:7). It's simple, but not easy. Sanctification requires diligent, strenuous, constant effort.

If we claim the righteousness of Christ in justification, then we must bear the righteous fruit of sanctification. They cannot be separated. John pulled no punches, unequivocally confessing, "By this the children of God and the children of the devil are obvious: anyone who does not practice righteousness is not of God, nor the one who does not love his brother" (3:10). Satan eschews righteousness; he despises it. Believers must imitate their Father and do what He desires (John 8:44). Christ was equally candid: "If you love Me, you will keep My commandments" (John 14:15). Thankfully, God graciously supplies believers with every resource required to accomplish His righteous purposes.

Properly Responding to Discipline

Speaking of straightforward Scripture, Proverbs doesn't beat around the bush either: "Whoever loves discipline loves knowledge, *but he who hates reproof is stupid*" (12:1, emphasis added). Ever convicting, this verse highlights the importance of our response to God's good discipline. In fact, our response is another useful indicator of our love for righteousness since He disciplines in order to make us holy. He accomplishes this through trials, working through people and circumstances to burn away our sin. Hebrews explains, "All discipline for the moment seems not to be joyful, but sorrowful; yet to those who have been trained by it, afterwards it yields the peaceful fruit of righteousness" (12:11). Just as a parent must bring physical discipline to bear on a young child for correction, God brings discipline in order to train us.

As a parent, I felt the achy longing for my own little children to learn from the painful consequences I was obliged to administer as a result of their willful disobedience. However, many times they would forget the punishment and immediately return to the behavior that brought the chastisement—over and over again. The cycle would regretfully continue. Many of us are in the same holding pattern with God. Are we fulfilling our role in learning? Are we allowing the painful correction to change our behavior? Or are we "a fool who repeats his folly . . . like a dog that returns to its vomit" (Prov. 26:11)? We somehow think we will find pleasure in returning to the muck God already guaranteed would give no fulfillment. Then we cry out to God, bewildered by His heavy hand upon us. Yet He lovingly reveals through His Word that we need His righteousness more than we need an easy life.

Put Off and Put On

In summary, we must seek to put away our sin and put on the corresponding righteous behavior. For example, Paul didn't merely command the Ephesians to no longer steal. He urged each person to "labor, performing with his own hands what is good, so that he will have something to share with one who has need" (Eph. 4:28). Do you see the difference? *The thief doesn't stop being a thief when he puts away his thievery; he stops being a thief only when he starts working for the benefit of others.* This is true of all sin.

Maybe a husband, for example, has finally exerted the self-control and patience needed to no longer habitually yell at his wife and kids. While the spirit of forbearance and restraint is godly, the man *fully* practices righteousness in this particular area when he speaks gracious, encouraging, gentle words to his family instead. We cannot simply put off and not put on. If we want to truly hunger and thirst for righteousness, we must be mindful to intentionally *put on*. This is discovered through the renewing of our minds by the truth of God's Word (Rom. 12:2).

The Reward

The reward for craving the right thing is satisfaction. The longing will be gratified. Christ promised that if we truly desire righteousness, He will grant it. He blesses us with a measure of satisfaction in this life as we daily pursue holiness, but also an eternal fulfillment with our resurrected bodies unstained by sin's filth. Spurgeon notes, "Where God works such an insatiable desire, we may be quite sure that He will satisfy it; yea, fill it to the brim."[8] As mentioned before, the desire never ceases, but in heaven there will be no barrier to a constant state of perpetual satisfaction to fill that desire. This satisfaction will primarily express itself in joy. David sang, "You have put gladness in my heart, more than when their grain and new wine abound" (Ps. 4:7). People would celebrate after the harvest by eating and drinking their fill, but David knew that didn't bring ultimate happiness. At our hotel resort in Hawaii, they created the same atmosphere. Sadly, for unbelievers, that's the height of life — good times through food and drink with good company, but those things are all temporal.

What a blessing that true joy comes through eternal and worthy pursuits like righteousness. If we lack joy, we are searching for it in the wrong place. Psalm 107 exclaims, "For He has satisfied the thirsty soul, and the hungry soul He has filled with what is good" (v. 9). We are fulfilled as we pursue holiness. This joy-inducing satisfaction is also secure; in fact, part of our contentment rests in knowing we drink from a fountain that will never, ever run dry. Because God is the source, the feast will never end. The food will never perish. In light of this, why would we ever consider what the world has to offer? God asks and answers:

> Why do you spend money for what is not bread,
> And your wages for what does not satisfy?

---

8. MacArthur, *Matthew* (1985), 183–184.

Listen carefully to Me, and eat what is good,
And delight yourself in abundance.
Incline your ear and come to Me.
Listen, that you may live. (Isa. 55:2–3)

~

Blest are the souls that thirst for grace,
hunger and long for righteousness;
they shall be well supplied, and fed
with living streams and living bread.

~Isaac Watts, 1709

Questions for Reflection & Discussion

1. Write down your memory of the hungriest you've ever been. Do the same for the thirstiest time you ever remember. Finally, recall a time you desperately desired God's holiness. What did you do, if anything, to solve each problem?

2. What does "holiness solves everything" mean?

3. Define righteousness.

4. Even as believers we can carve out "a space for idols in our hearts," but they can never offer true fulfillment. What idols do you tend to turn to for satisfaction? Why won't they ever fully meet that need? Why can God always meet that need?

5. Dulling our appetites for God, what trivial distractions (or plastic fruit) do we waste time on? List just one new habit that you could practice for a month to combat this.

6. Describe the righteousness required for kingdom entrance (justification).

7. Describe the righteousness necessary for kingdom living (sanctification).

8. What's the difference between the two? Why must they always go hand in hand? Do you see evidence of sanctification in your life? Do others?

9. Is there a growing divide between what you believe and what you do/not do? Prayerfully map out a plan to close this gap today in one specific area. What is standing in your way? How can you remove that obstacle?

10. Is there an area in your life where it seems you may be in a disciplinary holding pattern with God? What won't you learn? What biblical truth(s) will help you stop "returning to your vomit"?

11. List two ways to sharpen your appetite for righteousness. How will you specifically pursue these this week?

Chapter 6

Blessed Are the Merciful

Blessed are the merciful, for they shall receive mercy.

In nearly every adventure story, the climactic moment invariably arises when the hero and villain square off in a final showdown. The dastardly villain, overconfident in his malevolent abilities, dramatically approaches the hero with a settled smugness. The hero, gallantly championing the cause of right, engages in a battle culminating in the villain's defeat. Prostrate before him, the reckless wrongdoer pleads for what? *Mercy.* Stripped of everything, including his own ability to save himself, he determines that unmerited mercy is highly preferable to administered justice.

Man has a tendency to think justice should be meted out against others while withheld from himself. In fact, man in his natural condition doesn't desire to show mercy, not until he recognizes and understands his own need for it—until he is likewise stripped of his own abilities, self-righteousness, and self-sufficiency. We are often quickly angered with others and swift to bring their punishment, while unduly lenient with ourselves. We are in great need of possessing a godly mercy that understands the righteousness and reality of suffering for sin, yet longs to see others comforted and relieved from the dreadful consequences of it. *Every citizen of the kingdom is a grateful recipient of God's mercy and longs to see others rescued from the suffering and affliction caused by sin.*

We are advancing another step in our progression. Retracing our steps, we learned humility is required in order to perceive our own spiritual bankruptcy, understanding that a poor spirit recognizes there's nothing to offer in the eyes of a holy God. This lowly valuation, in turn, causes us to mourn over our sin rather than delighting in it and its means of sufficiency. We abandon our self-righteousness, lament over grieving God with our wickedness, and turn to Him empty-handed.

Next, we examined the cultivation of a spirit of gentleness by yielding our own will to His, allowing Him to take our yoke upon Himself. Instead of asserting our own will to gain that which we desire, we humble ourselves underneath Him as His desires direct our lives. As we ever more increasingly discern our own lack of innate righteousness, we enjoy an equally growing hunger and thirst for His. We desperately seek after it, knowing holiness solves everything. His imputed righteousness enables us to receive His mercy and is necessary for us to have a relationship with Him. Then, as we pursue sanctification, we are able to love Him more, deepening in our relationship as we minister to others.

Thus far, the beatitudes have dealt with inner characteristics of our spirit that have been building toward external expression. How will we demonstrate these internal heart attitudes that are both the means of entrance into the kingdom *and* the means by which we live within it? While the "first four beatitudes express in one way or another our dependence on God," the latter half will necessarily flow out of that dependence.[1] To the extent that we cultivate these inner attitudes we will bear the fruit of the remaining blessings as a direct consequence.

Defining Mercy

With that in mind, Jesus again promised blessedness. Like a litmus test for kingdom citizenship, the more we demonstrate these characteristics, the more we experience the benefits that accompany them. In verse 7, the guaranteed blessing for bestowing mercy is that we will receive mercy in return. So, what exactly is it? Since the world has one definition and God another, we must define it by His terms to ensure we aren't misunderstanding the very nature of that which we should be manifesting. As always, the definition will be tied to the character and nature of God.

Jesus commanded believers to "be merciful, just as your Father is merciful" (Luke 6:36). Thus, the mercy we must confer to others flows from God Himself. Empowered by Him, it is a reflection of His own mercy, which graciously withholds what we justly deserve. Mercy can be broadly defined as *the expression of love which causes us to have compassion on and actively help those who are suffering and afflicted, either due to their own sin or the sinfulness of the world in which we all live.* Mercy is simply compassion for those who suffer — a deep, affectionate love for those who are miserable. That misery can come as a result of their own sin or merely from living in a sin-cursed world. It is a sincere care for the hurt and pain others feel in their distress.

Sadly, we are slow to this kind of genuine concern, and we don't truly have any real measure of it apart from God's grace and our understanding of who He is. A more specific definition of God's mercy includes *deliverance from the rightful punishment of our sin on the basis*

---

1. Leon Morris, *The Gospel According to Matthew*, ed. D. A. Carson, *The Pillar New Testament Commentary* (Grand Rapids: Eerdmans, 1992), 100.

of the full payment provided by Christ. The world can only manufacture echoes of this kind of compassion; they can never fully embody it since they don't know God. We must first understand that people primarily suffer because of their own sin. The apostle Paul explained,

> But God, *being rich in mercy,* because of His great love with which He loved us, even when we were dead in our transgressions, made us alive together with Christ (by grace you have been saved), and raised us up with Him and seated us with Him in the heavenly places in Christ Jesus. (Eph. 2:4; emphasis added)

Essentially, men do not experience the full consequences of their own sinfulness in this life. They only receive reverberations of God's wrath, so to speak. His righteous judgment upon sin is experienced in this world by believers and unbelievers alike as a result of living in a fallen world. Our own sin, unworthiness, and unfaithfulness cause the greatest amount of suffering, and yet a holy God has mercy on us — *that is amazing.* God looks upon this self-inflicted pain and misery, whose very cause offends His perfect holiness, and yet longs to make provision for us!

We, on the other hand, are not so merciful. When we think others deserve the predicaments in which they find themselves, we are slow to desire their deliverance from the pain. Of course, we understand that those who don't know Christ will reap the bitter fullness of misery and affliction in eternal hell. We will consider God's temporal and eternal justice as it pertains to His mercy, but we must first recognize that God longs to deliver people from suffering. That is His heart's desire. He does not rejoice in man's misery, even as it exists as a necessary component of His righteous character. God is merciful. He delights in rescuing people from the hardship of their own making, so we must cultivate the same heartfelt response.

We must also pity those who are afflicted simply due to living in a world stained by sin in the broad sense, remembering that the general difficulties of life all find their origin in the fall of humanity. These difficulties are nonexistent in heaven where perfection abounds, and mercy is unnecessary. But because we live in a sinful world where others sin against us, we are in desperate need of God actually demonstrating His compassion.

Demonstrating Mercy — God

It is not only a heart of compassion, but as our definition states, a willingness and an actual working to alleviate the suffering of others. It is not only a stirring of the soul, but help — not merely affection, but action. Mercy does not just say, *I am so sorry for you.* It says, *I am so sorry for you, and I aim to fix it.* It's active. It renders aid to those afflicted by gracious and kind actions with the goal of providing relief.

A primary way in which God accomplishes this purpose is by keeping His promises, even though we're undeserving. This is an expression of His mercy. God is always faithful to honor His unconditional promises to unworthy people as an extension of His character. But it's astonishing that even in His conditional promises, when men wrestle to uphold the conditions, God still pours out His mercy on them.

Forgiveness to the unfaithful is also a chief demonstration of His mercy. In forgiving sin, God relieved us of its penalty because that's what forgiveness is — a pardon granted. No longer will we who have been forgiven suffer eternity in hell as a consequence of our sins committed against a holy God: "He saved us, not on the basis of deeds which we have done in righteousness, but according to His mercy by the washing of regeneration and renewal of the Holy Spirit" (Titus 3:5). Wholly based on Christ's sacrifice, this forgiveness is grounded in justice and truth, and yet mercy is enacted upon those who are entirely unworthy. We have brought our conditions upon ourselves, and God longs to relieve us from our misery. He meets this need by the ultimate actionable demonstration of sending His own Son to pay the price of the pardon. Again, mercy is not merely a heartfelt response that lapses into handwringing. Mercy acts. It sacrifices. It costs!

When God *fully* enacts mercy, it is eternal, but He also graciously provides temporal deliverance from circumstances to both believers and unbelievers alike. Christ demonstrated this continually during His earthly ministry. As He left Jericho and crowds surrounded Him, for example, two blind beggars cried out to Him, "Lord, have mercy on us, Son of David!" (Matt. 20:30). Christ was "moved with compassion" and healed them (20:34). Blindness in that day was essentially a death knell that reduced its sufferer to a lifetime of perpetual beggary. Yet Jesus brought His mercy to bear to deliver the needy from the source of their great temporal affliction. In this case, it appears they believed in Him, but the recipients of Christ's healing mercy didn't always turn and bow the knee. Even upon the unsaved who are at enmity with Him, God provides some mercy in withholding the fullness of the penalty by granting them a measure of relief in this life. This is the compassion of God, and it's how ours is to mirror.

Simple Mercy

Jesus bestowed this mercy again at the entrance of Nain with His disciples and a large crowd surrounding Him. Luke's gospel records, "Now as He approached the gate of the city, a dead man was being carried out, the only son of his mother, and she was a widow; and a sizeable crowd from the city was with her" (7:12). This wasn't just a chance encounter, even though it's framed as almost coincidental that Christ arrived at the precise moment this woman and her deceased son passed by with their own throng. The widow, already bereft of her husband, had now lost her dearest and only source of provision. She was afflicted, suffering, and left weeping in the midst of her tragic circumstances. When their paths crossed, Jesus "felt compassion for her, and said to her, 'Do not weep'" (7:13). He didn't simply walk by her, even though widows abounded in Israel. He saw her condition and stopped, sincerely affected by her plight. He didn't have to drum up sympathy; rather, His instantaneous desire flowed from His very heart.

After such a curious and jarring injunction to the woman, He walked over and "touched the coffin; and the bearers came to a halt" (7:14). Preventing the coffin from being carried further, He issued an even more astonishing command: "Young man, I say to you, arise!" (7:14). The young man instantaneously responded by both sitting up and speaking, and then Christ "gave him back to his mother" (7:15). Why did He do that? The text never states that they followed Him necessarily, yet Christ desired to alleviate the misery of this woman who would fully experience the consequences of her son's death for the rest of her life. Fear gripping the crowds, they all celebrated, "glorifying God" (7:16). But it seems they were more amazed by the miraculous deliverance from death than they were by the astounding compassion that drove such deliverance. We too often revel in God's mighty power without giving equal weight to His great compassion, nor do we recognize the necessity of imitating it.

The Need for Mercy

Mercy is the opposite of God's wrath. Even though we deserve the latter, in Christ we receive the former instead. Because we are the recipients of this great salvific mercy, we are now individually empowered and required to extend God's mercy to others rather than directing personal indignation toward them. We are all in great need of His mercy to gain admission into the kingdom because Scripture is abundantly clear that we deserve His wrath:

> And you were dead in your trespasses and sins, in
> which you formerly walked according to the course
> of this world, according to the prince of the power of
> the air, of the spirit that is now working in the sons of
> disobedience. Among them we too all formerly lived

in the lusts of our flesh, indulging the desires of the flesh and of the mind, and were by nature children of wrath, even as the rest. (Eph. 2:1–3)

God rightfully pours out His holy fury upon sin. We have warranted it, so we are in desperate need of His great mercy. We must be rescued from His just and perfect wrath.

Fascinatingly, there are several words used in the original biblical languages to reference this concept of mercy. One Greek word relates to the mercy seat, the place above the ark of the covenant where blood was sprinkled during Old Covenant sacrifices to seek God's forgiveness (Heb. 9:5). In fact, the primary use of "mercy" in the Old Testament refers to this precious seat upon which "the faces of the cherubim are to be turned toward" (Exod. 25:20). The application of sacrificial blood prefigured Christ's death that cleansed us from our sin and relieved us from the painful misery of the eternal hell we so rightly deserved. Mercy still remains the place upon which we cry out for God's forgiveness. God's wrath poured out on His own Son, our great Deliverer, is the basis upon which He extends His mercy to us. And while this is certainly bound up in His justice, it's crucial to see the cross as driven by His own merciful character.

God bestows mercy out of delight, not of obligation. There is nothing inherent within us that compels God to provide this salvation and forgiveness. Rather, He longs and loves to grant mercy, and so He sent His Son. His mercy is required for us to enter into the kingdom; otherwise, we must suffer the consequences of our sin. In His Sermon on the Mount, Christ deemed those blessed who, because they have received mercy, live out that mercy. It's needed because we and others still sin and fail. Sin and its ravages still remain even within the kingdom as we live here on earth. We are all in continual need of mercy, both vertically from God and horizontally with others. Until Christ returns to finalize His kingdom, we will all suffer within the cruelty of a fallen world of sin. But this also means opportunities for us to extend mercy and alleviate misery abound. Because of the mercy we have been granted to enter into the kingdom, we should long to richly bestow it on everyone around us. We must cultivate a heart of mercy.

The Heart of Mercy

What does this transformed heart look like? Developing these inner heart attitudes will determine our level of success in obediently living out this command to be merciful.

Love

First, mercy flows from love, so we must foster a heart of love. Paul stated that God is "rich in mercy, because of His great love" (Eph. 2:4). God extends mercy because He is a God of love. He delights to see us in loving relationships because He takes pleasure in drawing us into a loving relationship with Himself. This brings the greatest glory to both Christ and the Father. His love drives His joy in delivering us from the consequences of sin. John MacArthur carefully distinguishes between the two:

> Mercy is the physician; love is the friend. Mercy acts because of need; love acts because of affection, whether there is need or not. Mercy is reserved for times of trouble; love is constant. There can be no true mercy apart from love, but there can be true love apart from mercy.[2]

2. John MacArthur, *Matthew 1–7*, vol. 1, *The MacArthur New Testament Commentary* (Chicago: Moody Press, 1985), 191.

There will be no need of mercy in heaven because sin and suffering will be absent, but love will always remain.

However, for believers still sojourning in this sin-stained world, love motivates our mercy. In fact, gauging our compassion toward others is an accurate measuring stick of our love for them. Does our love prompt us to see *everyone* delivered from pain and difficulty? Do we delight to see all people in right relationship with God? To see them conformed to Christ's image? They are all in urgent need of vast doses of mercy, and our love should propel us to generously administer the medicine.

Humility

Humility of heart is also essential if we are to exercise mercy. We must possess a willingness to understand and live according to the true lowliness of our actual state. Humility is antithetical to self-righteousness and self-sufficiency. It has undergirded the beatitudes thus far: poorness of spirit, mournfulness over sin, gentleness, and a hunger and thirst for righteousness all require humility to recognize our own ignoble state in light of our perfect and holy God. We will grow in mercy to the degree we grow in humility. The converse is also true. In fact, the Pharisees offered the best illustration of a self-righteous lack of humility that prevented them from extending mercy. Their pride embodied their total failure to demonstrate real compassion for sinners. They didn't grant it because they didn't believe they were in need of it themselves. They lived according to the law. They kept the law, they made the proper sacrifices, and so they earned their admission into the kingdom, or so they thought.

When Jesus was spending time with tax collectors and sinners, pouring out His mercy upon those undeserved, the Pharisees were appalled and questioned His disciples. Upon hearing their disgust, Jesus retorted, "Go and learn what this means: 'I DESIRE COMPASSION AND NOT SACRIFICE,' for I did not come to call the righteous, but sinners"

(Matt. 9:13). Christ implied that God rejected their sacrifices before the altar because they were devoid of mercy; and they were merciless to others because of their confidence that they had earned their right standing before God. But Jesus was not truly classifying them as righteous—in fact, He condemned them. He declared that God only awards mercy to those who recognize their need for it, and the Pharisees with their arrogant self-righteousness and empty sacrifices refused to admit their need.

When we detect pride lurking in our own hearts, it's a symptom that we are not developing a heart of mercy as Christ desires. Do we truly recognize what He's done for us—that we have absolutely no sufficiency in ourselves; that He has poured out mercy upon us despite deserving nothing but hell; and that He graciously saved us at the expense of His own Son's life? In light of that, why are we so slow to pour it out upon others, especially upon those we are convinced don't deserve it? As we deepen in love and humility, we will increasingly grow in our expressions of mercy.

Compassion

We must also cultivate a compassionate heart that is easily moved with tender concern toward those who are in distress. This can be challenging as we are not always naturally moved to this when others are struggling. We tend to either focus on the deservedness of consequences reaped *or* minimize the hardship and determine the misery is blown out of proportion. But that indicates an arrogance of heart and a lack of love and compassion. The more we grow in Christ by His grace, the more we should be genuinely moved by the plight of others to alleviate their pain.

We need compassion not only for those who suffer the devastation of material difficulties and physical illnesses but for those who suffer spiritually. Sadly, we often lean toward having more pity for a person's dire situation in life than for his spiritual condition. We ought to feel the weight of those who are headed for eternal hell regardless of their worldly circumstances. Looking to His endless compassion as our standard of care, we must rely on the Lord to build this within us as we take hold of the resources He has provided by faith.

King David understood this difference between God's character and ours. When David decreed a census to number his people in direct opposition to God's will, the prophet Gad came to declare the ensuing punishment. Interestingly, God allowed David to "pick his poison," so to speak, from among three judgments: seven years of famine, three months of fleeing from enemies, or three days of pestilence. David's answer is remarkable: "I am in great distress. Let us now fall into the hand of the LORD for His mercies are great, but do not let me fall into the hand of man" (2 Sam. 24:14). Even though he knew God could exact infinitely more destruction, David also knew men would show no mercy, or at least nothing compared to God's abundant mercies. David's wisdom was vindicated as God brought pestilence upon the land, but as the appointed angel approached Jerusalem to devastate it, He relented and stayed his hand to spare the city. God was moved with compassion, even though both David and his city didn't deserve any. By the Spirit's power, believers must pursue that same heart.

Justice

Lastly and perhaps surprisingly, a heart of justice is necessary in order to truly bestow mercy. Justice properly understood is what distinguishes biblical mercy from the world's weak and cheap concept. The world's mercy has no accurate appraisal of sin and injustice. Their solution is to just "try to let it go." They don't want to be judged themselves, so they skirt justice in toto. Armed with a flimsy moral relativism rather than the Spirit's power, they can only attempt to drum up a sense of pity. If people inflict suffering on themselves or others, requiring a penalty can be considered overly harsh, even though people rarely feel that way when *they* are the victims of targeted offenses. Perhaps this is why recently, our society is abandoning mercy altogether in many arenas of public life, forsaking grace and forgiveness toward anyone who violates their ever-encroaching and ever-changing moral systems that are bound up in an utterly distorted sense of justice.

Paul pointed out that God "shut up all in disobedience so that He may show mercy to all" (Rom. 11:32). *There is no true mercy if there is no actual justice.* If things aren't actually wrong, then delivering people from consequences isn't even mercy anymore. It's reduced to merely our own arbitrary whims which carry no value. It is hollow, empty, and ultimately false. In reality, there is right, wrong, and real punishment that makes mercy possible. The deliverance from the rightful consequences of our sin is on the basis of justice paid in Christ. That's what makes mercy valuable. It is based upon the death of the Son of God. *True mercy is always costly*:

> The truth is that God does not show mercy without punishing sin; and for Him to offer mercy without punishment would negate His justice. Mercy that ignores sin is a false mercy and is no more merciful than it is just.[3]

This false mercy is common in our day. Holding people responsible for their sin is considered unloving and unkind by many, but this is cheap mercy. It is neither just nor merciful in that it offers neither punishment nor pardon for sin. Because sin is merely overlooked, sin remains. To abolish justice is to eradicate mercy alongside it. Psalm 85:10 assures, "Lovingkindness and truth have met together; righteousness and peace have kissed each other." The Hebrew term for "lovingkindness," *hesed*, is often translated as "mercy." True mercy is grounded in culpability for sin. God's delight in bestowing His mercy

---

3. MacArthur, *Matthew* (1985), 192.

upon the sinner came at the price of His Son's life. In every true act of mercy, someone pays the price—as Christ did.

Demonstrating Mercy—Us

How do we exercise this mercy-driven heart as kingdom citizens? What will it look like for us? It may be easy to sympathize with a sufferer, but remember that mercy acts! It's only true mercy when we are willing to give of ourselves and expend our resources to mitigate another's misery. Jesus' story of the Good Samaritan illustrates the price it cost to shower mercy upon a man in great affliction and need (Luke 10:35-37). Like the selfless Samaritan, to be merciful is to bear the load for someone else. Paralleling our Beatitude, the prophet Micah declares:

> He has told you, O man, what is good;
> And what does the LORD require of you
> But to do justice, to love kindness (or *mercy*),
> And to walk humbly with your God. (Mic. 6:8, parentheses added)

With that in mind, let's examine seven areas where we can practice extending godly mercy.

Forgiveness

We primarily demonstrate mercy through forgiveness. God's mercy toward us flows out in forgiveness toward others. The very essence of mercy is to forgive; it's how we are rescued from the penalty of sin and the misery it brings. Yet when our cold, harsh hearts secretly delight in seeing others suffer for their sin, it hinders our ability to forgive. This holds true in every kind of relationship where forgiveness is denied or delayed until we determine the offender has sufficiently suffered. We dwell on the offense—*Look at what he's done to me! I can't forgive him until he suffers first, or else my pain is discounted and devalued.* But mercy thinks, *Even though it hurts, I can't wait to forgive. What can I do to help alleviate him from the painful consequences of his actions?* Yes, it's grounded in justice and truth, and no, it's not cheap or easy, but it is essential. We should instantly forgive and stand ready to reconcile, always searching for ways to help. We choose to forgive in our hearts on the basis of what Christ has done for us. Holding bitterness against others in our hearts only wounds ourselves. Instead, we are commanded to forgive them because we long to see them relieved from the consequences of their own sin.

Later on in Jesus' sermon, He taught: "For if you forgive others for their transgressions, your heavenly Father will also forgive you. But if you do not forgive others, then your Father will not forgive your transgressions" (Matt. 6:14–15). Similar to the construction of our beatitude of mercy, neither statement claims

> we can merit mercy by mercy or forgiveness by forgiveness, but because we cannot receive the mercy and forgiveness of God unless we repent, and we cannot claim to have repented of our sins if we are unmerciful towards the sins of others. …Nothing proves more clearly that we have been forgiven than our own readiness to forgive. To forgive and to be forgiven, to show mercy and to receive mercy: these belong indissolubly together, as Jesus illustrated in his parable of the unmerciful servant.[4]

In Matthew 18, when Peter inquired of Christ the limit of our forgiveness, Christ expanded upon His answer of "seventy times seven" with a powerful parable (18:22):

---

4. John R. W. Stott, *The Message of the Sermon on the Mount*, rev. ed. (Downers Grove: Intervarsity Press, 2020), 31.

For this reason the kingdom of heaven may be compared to a king who wished to settle accounts with his slaves. When he had begun to settle them, one who owed him ten thousand talents was brought to him. But since he did not have the means to repay, his lord commanded him to be sold, along with his wife and children and all that he had, and repayment to be made. So the slave fell to the ground and prostrated himself before him, saying, "Have patience with me and I will repay you everything." And the lord of that slave felt compassion and released him and forgave him the debt. (Matt. 18:23–27)

The illustration showcases the compassion and great mercy of the master. As the helpless slave cravenly begged for forgiveness, promising that he would pay when he clearly couldn't, the master granted total forgiveness on the basis of his own merciful nature, not on what the slave could do. Christ continued:

But that slave went out and found one of his fellow slaves who owed him a hundred denarii; and he seized him and began to choke him, saying, "Pay back what you owe." So his fellow slave fell to the ground and began to plead with him, saying, "Have patience with me and I will repay you." But he was unwilling and went and threw him in prison until he should pay back what was owed. So when his fellow slaves saw what had happened, they were deeply grieved and came and reported to their lord all that had happened. Then summoning him, his lord said to him, "You wicked slave, I forgave you all that debt because you pleaded with me. Should you not also have had mercy on your fellow slave, in the same way that I had mercy on you?" (18:28–33)

This striking parable reveals our hearts when we fail to forgive anyone of anything. We cannot excuse our lack of forgiveness ever. There is nothing that we cannot pardon when we've been forgiven infinitely greater than the harm any sin against ourselves could ever inflict. We will not get our "pound of flesh" nor harbor any bitterness, but instead worship God for the rest of our lives because He did not withhold His forgiveness from us. We have a true foundation on which to offer that forgiveness because God deals with sin. Those who harm others will have either had Christ pay the penalty for their sin as a believer, or will face the consequences of their sin eternally as an unbeliever. We are therefore freed up to simply forgive knowing God will deal with them according to their ultimate condition.

Generosity

Secondly, true mercy will always result in selfless generosity. Because it longs to see people liberated from difficulty, mercy is characterized by the joyful, gracious giving of both spiritual and physical resources. Sometimes a greater problem lies in learning *how* to appropriately allocate these resources according to biblical principles and parameters; but our hearts should still echo the sentiment: *If I could provide you with everything, I would in a heartbeat. In fact, it grieves me that I can't give you more.* How often do our hearts yearn in this manner? Perhaps it can be at times toward the people we love most dearly, but maybe not when they sin against us; or surely not toward others with whom we have no relationship; and definitely not to others still who we've determined have fully deserved their comeuppance. Our hearts should overflow with a generosity that's only rightfully constrained by biblical wisdom.

We give according to Scripture, which undoubtedly encompasses spiritual needs. Lavishly "bless[ing] us with every spiritual blessing in the heavenly places in Christ" (Eph. 1:3), God provides in line with His generous nature. Applied to us at salvation and given to us through His Word, this abundant grace renders us conduits that bring

Scripture to bear in others' lives. Christ exemplified this throughout His ministry. On one occasion, as He "saw a large crowd . . . He felt compassion for them because they were like sheep without a shepherd; and He began to teach them many things" (Mark 6:34). We pour out our time, effort, and energy to bring the truth of God's Word to people in desperate spiritual need all around us—to the poor, struggling, and hopeless, and to the rich, self-sufficient, and self-righteous—because that's how a heart of mercy responds to need.

In the parallel account to Mark 6, Matthew mentioned that Christ also met purely physical needs; again, He beheld the crowd "and felt compassion for them and healed their sick" (Matt. 14:14). He didn't just teach them; He healed them. Christ cared for the whole person, as demonstrated by His recognition of a crowd's hunger on another occasion: "I feel compassion for the people because they have remained with me now three days and have nothing to eat; and I don't want to a send them away hungry, for they might faint on the way" (Matt. 15:32). Sincerely moved by their plight, He provided them deliverance from their physical deprivation, and we should long to do the same. As we minister to various material needs, though, we must bring spiritual resources to bear, so man's greater problem of impending eternal doom is addressed.

Judgment

Merciful judgment should also be part of our lives "for judgment will be merciless to one who has shown no mercy; mercy triumphs over judgment" (James 2:13). This depicts the negative corollary to our current Beatitude. If we refuse to accord mercy to others who deserve judgment, then God will withhold mercy to us who deserve the same verdict: "The merciful man does himself good, but the cruel man does himself harm" (Prov. 11:17). This doesn't mean we suspend proper evaluation in accordance with Scripture, nor does it mean we never bring penalties to bear for the violation of God's principles. It simply means we do everything appropriately possible to relieve others from the harmful consequences of their actions. For unbelievers, that ultimately manifests in a call to repentance and faith. The Bible commends righteous judgment but condemns unmerciful judgment. We confuse the two far too often, so we must exercise great care in distinguishing one from the other. We must remember that God is continually extending mercy toward us on every level, and we should never become more demanding than He is.

Evangelism

The ministry of presenting the truth of the gospel to those who are suffering and dying from the affliction of sin is the utmost display of mercy. Speaking of this "manifestation of truth," Paul testified, "Since we have this ministry, as we have received mercy, we do not lose heart" (2 Cor. 4:2; 1). He proclaimed, "Yet for this reason I found mercy, so that in me as the foremost [of sinners], Jesus Christ might demonstrate His perfect patience as an example for those who would believe in Him for eternal life" (1 Tim. 1:16). Because we've been shown mercy through the gospel, we have the privilege of sharing the message with others. We proclaim the good news that "in the shedding of Christ's blood justice was satisfied, sin was forgiven, righteousness was fulfilled, and mercy was made available."[5] There is always a remedy for sin, and our mercy drives us to readily present that antidote until our dying breath.

Comfort

The merciful heart loves to bring comfort to those who are in distress. Paul declared,

> Blessed be the God and Father of our Lord Jesus Christ, the Father of mercies and God of all comfort, who comforts us in all our affliction so that we will

---

5. MacArthur, *Matthew* (1985), 193.

be able to comfort those who are in any affliction
with the comfort with which we ourselves have been
comforted by God. (2 Cor. 1:3–4)

Lending comfort is not exclusive to those who tend to have nurturing personalities. Mercy is "more than an instinct, more than a sentiment, more than the natural answer of the human heart to the sight of compassion and distress."[6] Even if one feels he is not predisposed with a compassionate personality, he is empowered by the Spirit to comfort others in pain. We are all called to this ministry.

Comfort can be easy to offer those who treat us well, but it can become a challenge when they sin against us. As a parent, when I'm convinced my child is fully deserving of the righteous judgment I'm administering, it can be hard to give comfort after bringing physical discipline to bear if I haven't dealt with my own sin against him. On more than one occasion, my subsequent "comfort" was as artificial as a child's reaction when told to go and hug his sister — a robotic, insincere, and empty gesture. Aren't we so thankful that's not how God treats us? We must repent and remind ourselves of the "comfort with which we ourselves have been comforted by God" (1:4). This comfort informs and motivates our own.

Patience

The heart of mercy is longsuffering with others due to the strong desire to deliver them from pain. This is God's heart: "But you, O Lord, are a God merciful and gracious, slow to anger and abundant in lovingkindness and truth" (Ps. 86:15). Even though God's righteous anger burns, He is slow to bring about the consequences. He delays as long as possible according to His great patience so that people may be rescued from both temporal and eternal consequences. Contrary to popular belief, the Old Testament is rife with God's compassion

---

6. Alexander Maclaren, *The Gospel According to St. Matthew* (New York: A. C. Armstrong & Son, 1905), 148.

and patience exercised not only toward His chosen nation, but outsiders as well. The wickedness that arose from Nineveh roused God to send Jonah to call them to repentance rather than immediately obliterate the city. While patient with the ruthless society, God also demonstrated forbearance with His own prophet who spurned the mercy extended to his enemy. God patiently schooled Jonah on His great compassion (Jon. 4:3–11).

The New Testament continues in eulogizing God's great patience. Peter clarified that the Lord is in no way lacking righteousness when we perceive reluctance on His part to judge; instead, He is "patient toward [the world], not wishing for any to perish but all to come to repentance" (2 Pet. 3:9). Since God's anger is always righteous, how much more should we be slow to our anger that so often is tainted with sin? We forbear and prolong anger, so we can first dispense mercy.

Prayer

Finally, we demonstrate a heart of mercy by continually bringing others before God in prayer, beseeching the Lord on their behalf, so that they would drink deeply from the well of His mercy. Hebrews exhorts us to "draw near with confidence to the throne of grace, so that we may receive mercy and find grace to help in time of need" (4:16). Do you regularly bring others before God's throne in prayer? Do you pray for them to receive the mercy that only God can administer? We must recognize that He dispenses it to others through us, so we must be faithful to pray.

The Reward

As with each Beatitude, a reward always follows: "Blessed are the merciful, for they shall receive mercy." This is not mercy from men since we are in no way guaranteed that others will reciprocate when we bestow mercy upon them. In fact, oftentimes the more merciful we are, the weaker we appear to the world and the greater its desire to exploit us. But not to Christ. Our mercy-giving is only a reflection of our kingdom citizenship. It doesn't initiate or compel God to return mercy; rather, it's an expression that we've recognized and responded to the mercy He has first granted to us. It's assurance that as our lives pour out mercy, we are truly in the kingdom and will one day receive the full benefit of that mercy — eternity in heaven with the triune God.

~

Blest are the men whose hearts do move
and melt with sympathy and love;
from Christ the Lord shall they obtain
like sympathy and love again.

~Isaac Watts, 1709

Questions for Reflection & Discussion

1. What is mercy?

2. Generally speaking, why do people suffer?

3. Define forgiveness. How is it a kind of mercy?

4. From any of the gospels, give two examples of Christ demonstrating mercy.

5. List several reasons believers should exercise mercy toward others.

6. What is the relationship between mercy and the cross? Meditate on this idea.

7. What are obstacles that prevent you from exercising mercy? What biblical truths help you to overcome these hindrances?

8. Are you a naturally compassionate person? Why is this largely irrelevant for the believer?

9. Describe the relationship between justice and mercy. Meditate on this.

10. Mercy is most challenging to give when we are sinned against. Detail a plan below in both thought and action to prepare in advance.

Chapter 7

Blessed Are the Pure in Heart

Blessed are the pure in heart, for they shall see God.

M y family and I live about twenty-five miles from Oak Ridge, Tennessee. Known as "The Secret City," this small town was created in 1942 by the United States government. Their top-secret mission known as the Manhattan Project had one express purpose—build an atomic bomb. While the production of this weapon of mass destruction in 1944–45 played a significant role in the course of World War II, the invention was made possible by scientific discoveries in nuclear physics dating back to the 1800s.[1] Understanding the inner workings of the atom's nucleus laid the foundation to develop the bomb. Until scientists learned how the heart of the atom functioned, they couldn't unleash the energy it contained.

---

1. Richard Rhodes, *The Making of the Atomic Bomb* (New York: Simon & Schuster, 1986).

Similarly, believers need a true, biblical understanding of their own hearts. As we understand how our hearts operate and are impacted by God's Word, we can more effectively "unleash" holiness in our lives. The Bible is the sole source from which God enables and empowers this purity. The truth contained in His Word internally transforms us from the heart before flowing out into external actions. Everything we desire, will, think, feel, and do is informed by the heart. *For believers, life in God's kingdom requires a continual growth in purity as a demonstration of the reality of our changed hearts and renewed lives.*

Our previous chapter introduced the latter beatitudes as the external outflowing of the heart attitudes cultivated in the first half. Our needy, repentant, yielding souls that desperately desire God's holiness graduate to outward expression in merciful actions toward others and, as we will see in this chapter, righteous conduct stemming from an ever-increasing purity of heart. In fact, purity of heart manifested in sanctified living is a direct application of the hungering and thirsting for righteousness addressed in this passage.

The resultant growth in holiness never stops for the kingdom citizen. This endurance is referred to as the *perseverance of the saints.* Those who have bona fide kingdom citizenship will grow in purity because the Spirit of God resides within them. As a consequence of that indwelling, believers possess an inexorable, internal gravitation toward holiness. Every true Christian is driven to holiness as certain as a living organism is driven to grow. It's part and parcel of who they are. Just as an organism that doesn't grow is dead, so too is the faith of a professing believer who does not pursue righteousness. So, what exactly is purity of heart?

Defining Purity of Heart

The Greek phrase transliterates as *katharos ho kardia.* We can easily recognize *kardia* as "heart" from *cardiovascular* or *cardiology,* but the term for "pure" may be recognized as well from the word *catharsis*, which references a kind of purification. The Greek term in our text is defined as being clean and free from corrupted desire and sin's guilt.[2] The term was often used in reference to metals "that had been refined until all impurities were removed, leaving only the pure metal," rendering them "unmixed, unalloyed, [and] unadulterated."[3] Used to describe the heart, the term likewise represented "single-mindedness, undivided devotion, spiritual integrity and true righteousness."[4] It refers to believers who are entirely free from the guilt of sin and ever increasingly from its presence.

Biblically defined, the heart is vastly more encompassing than our culture's understanding. It's not simply emotion. God's Word describes the heart as the control center of the entire inner person. It comprises the mind, will, conscience, and affections, along with our personalities that individually distinguish us. The Bible may interchangeably use terms such as *heart, soul, mind,* or *spirit,* but the reference is always to our inner being. Scripture views the heart from many different angles. While one text may focus on the intellect and reason, another may be placed in the context of the passions and affections. Combined, the heart is the "seat of man's collective energies, the focus of personal life, the seat of the rational as well as the emotional and volitional elements in human life."[5] In short, the heart is really all that we are on the inside; it's "the 'real' you, . . . the essential core of who you are."[6]

Putting our terms together, the phrase sounds familiar. But contrary to popular fairytale lore, *pure of heart* refers not to a valiant,

2. W. E. Vine, *Vine's Complete Expository Dictionary of Old and New Testament Words* (Nashville: Thomas Nelson, 1996), 169.
3. John MacArthur, *Matthew 1–7,* vol. 1, *The MacArthur New Testament Commentary* (Chicago: Moody Press, 1985), 201.
4. MacArthur, *Matthew* (1985), 201.
5. George Abbott-Smith, *A Manual Greek Lexicon of the New Testament* (New York: Continuum Books, 1999), 230.
6. Paul David Tripp, *Instruments in the Redeemer's Hands* (Phillipsburg, New Jersey: P&R, 2002), 59.

quest-bound knight courageously seeking to vanquish the mighty foe and rescue the fair maiden. Instead, purity must characterize every aspect of the heart mentioned. We seek to be pure in our thinking and pure in our desires, pure in our conscience and pure in our affections. *Purity of heart, thus, is the single-minded, sincere devotion to God flowing from a heart that has been washed and renewed by the Holy Spirit and which results in the passionate practice of holiness.*

This beatitude focuses on the actual exercise of righteousness, not just hungering and thirsting for it. Christians don't merely wish to be holy; through the Holy Spirit's indwelling, they are enabled to actually demonstrate holiness. Kingdom citizens are equipped to accomplish what their King commands of them. Unlike the Pharisees, this is not external moralism, but rightly motivated godly living.

The Need for Purity of Heart

As with every other Beatitude, a pure heart is not only required for kingdom living, but also necessary for entrance: "Jesus demands purity [in the heart]. To be pure in heart is to be pure throughout."[7] However, men are in need of a heart transplant because every single person has a dead and depraved heart. God declared, "The heart is more deceitful than all else and is desperately sick; who can understand it?" (Jer. 17:9). Before salvation, our hearts are "perpetual factor[ies] of idols" from which only rebellion and lawlessness emerge.[8] By definition, this stained, corrupted heart does not have the capacity to attain purity. A pure heart can only be produced by God's Word through the Spirit's transforming power on the basis of the person and work of Jesus Christ.

---

7. Leon Morris, *The Gospel According to Matthew*, ed. D. A. Carson, *The Pillar New Testament Commentary* (Grand Rapids: Eerdmans, 1992), 65.
8. John Calvin, *Institutes of the Christian Religion*, I.11.8 (Peabody, MA: Hendrickson, 2008).

The Pharisees were no exception to this universal problem of mankind. Christ clearly described their dilemma. While they were confident that righteous purity could be gained by external, moral conformity, their hearts remained as dead as ever. They were arrogantly self-righteous, as if dirty, sinful, deceitful hearts were capable of producing purity. Christ vociferously condemned them:

> Woe to you, scribes and Pharisees, hypocrites! For you clean the outside of the cup and of the dish, but inside they are full of robbery and self-indulgence. You blind Pharisee, first clean the inside of the cup and of the dish, so that the outside of it may become clean also. Woe to you, scribes and Pharisees, hypocrites! For you are like whitewashed tombs which on the outside appear beautiful, but inside they are full of dead men's bones and all uncleanness. So you, too, outwardly appear righteous to men, but inwardly you are full of hypocrisy and lawlessness. (Matt. 23:25-28)

Whereas hypocrisy is marked by division and a lack of integrity, a pure heart is single-mindedly focused and sincere. The unconverted heart *must* be changed. Christ pointed out that trying to clean up the outside is worthless because the inner man is already defiled: "But the things that proceed out of the mouth come from the heart, and those defile the man. For out of the heart come evil thoughts, murders, adulteries, fornications, thefts, false witness, slanders. These are the things which defile the man" (Matt. 15:18-20).

The worst, most unspeakable depravities of man emanate from within himself, and yet the world insists all people are fundamentally good at heart. They routinely point to evil originating outside of men, blaming the culture, for example, even though culture is a direct reflection of men's hearts. Unsurprisingly, philosophers and world religions entirely miss this most basic point because they blindly and willfully "suppress the truth in unrighteousness" (Rom. 1:18). The world refuses to accept the premise that evil flows out of the human heart by its very nature—such an unpleasant truth would overturn their schemes to display their own goodness.

Men pridefully esteem themselves too highly to confess such debasement; and neither do they want to abandon the throne of their own desires for a subservient role in another's kingdom. Instead, they devote their resources to reforming society—changing governmental systems, dismantling traditional institutions, standardizing educational policies. If the environment could be calibrated just right, they assert, people would flourish on their own since they are essentially good. Such a theory is morally insane, but men would rather pursue it with their entire lives than bend the knee to Christ. Through Christ and the gospel, God accomplishes what men with dead hearts cannot do: produce new, living hearts that are pure and worthy of kingdom citizenship.

Like the other beatitudes thus far, purity of heart is necessary both to enter the kingdom *and* to live within it as a faithful citizen. Let's first consider the need for purity to enter His kingdom: Paul taught, "He saved us, not on the basis of deeds which we have done in righteousness, but according to His mercy, by the washing of regeneration and renewing by the Holy Spirit" (Titus 3:5). At salvation, the Spirit convicts a person's heart with the truths of God's Word, purifying and regenerating it, so that the person repents and believes.

Paul clarified, "Therefore if anyone is in Christ, he is a new creature; the old things passed away; behold, new things have come" (2 Cor. 5:17). God described the process as "tak[ing] the heart of stone (a dead heart) out of their flesh and giv[ing] them a heart of flesh (a living heart), that they may walk in [His] statutes and keep [His] ordinances and do them" (Ezek. 11:19–20, parentheses added). The Spirit imparts purity at salvation—we "draw near with a sincere heart in full assurance of faith, having our hearts sprinkled clean from an evil conscience and our bodies washed with pure water" (Heb. 10:22).

Second, as a part of our sanctification, or practical holiness, as discussed in chapter 5, we pursue purity of heart to function effectively *within* the kingdom. We flourish as a believer when we pursue this purity. As we partner with the Spirit, He empowers us to give outward expression to the purification wrought in our inner man. The purity that results from a renewed, clean heart is revealed ever increasingly as the remaining sin is gradually burned away.

In fact, sin's presence in our lives muddies up and obscures the clear view of this utterly changed heart. Believers can feel so bogged down with the "sin which so easily entangles" (Heb. 12:1), the idea of their hearts actually being clean might seem far-fetched. The remaining sin that resides in the inner man, however, is no longer who we are. Though it can detrimentally impact our hearts, it is now an intruder.

Consider the illustration of a corrupt, evil totalitarian state. The domineering regime is toppled, and a new, honest and upright government is installed to run the country. Those deposed officials, however, wage guerilla warfare against the new administration through an insurgency that seeks to subvert and resist. They operate a complex network of terrorist sleeper cells across the state. Through sophisticated espionage, they can detect any weakness and activate specific cells so as to constantly harass the new government. Battles and skirmishes are recurring, and the new government, though unquestioningly more powerful, must still be in a constant state of vigilance and be prepared to defend (or preemptively attack) at a moment's notice. Unlike conventional warfare, the enemy never concedes and retreats back to its own nation. The battle is internal and perpetual; such is the battle that wages within the heart of a believer, even as the heart's core has been transformed.

The believer must also contend with enemies on the external front. In this theater of war, the world as it's controlled by Satan assaults us right at our borders (1 John 5:19). This means that although Satan does not enter the believer's inner man in any way, he cunningly tempts the indwelling flesh to sin through every external means at his disposal in the world. To fight the war on both fronts, then, we must set up forces on each side of the heart, guarding from both "internal corruption" and "external influences."[9] Proverbs exhorts, "Watch over your heart with all diligence, for from it flow the springs of life" (4:23). *We must carefully watch over what tries to gain influence over our hearts apart from the Word of God, whether it be a threat from the outside or the inside.* Our hearts remain in need of refinement. Paul implored, "Therefore, having these promises, beloved, let us cleanse ourselves from all defilement of flesh and spirit, perfecting holiness in the fear of God" (2 Cor. 7:1). This is our sanctification we must relentlessly pursue. This is the "already, but not yet" state in which believers live and to which the apostle frequently referred: renewed, and yet renewing; pure, and yet being purified.

When we pursue this holiness, Christ promises we will see God. We will dive into this reward at the end of the chapter, but we must understand the link between our holiness and seeing Him in *His* holiness. Our growth in purity of heart demonstrates our citizenship in the present form of the kingdom, but it also guarantees that we will see the King in His glorious majesty when He returns again:

> See how great a love the Father has bestowed on us, that we would be called children of God; and such we are. For this reason the world does not know us, because it did not know Him. Beloved, now we are children of God, and it has not appeared as yet what we will be. We know that when He appears, we will be like Him, because we will see Him just as He is. And everyone who has this hope fixed on Him purifies himself, just as He is pure. (1 John 3:1–3)

---

9. Yvonne Hanson, *Rare: A Young Woman Who Fears the Lord* (Akron: 48 Hour Books, 2012), 14.

Our growth in purity of heart confirms we will gaze on Him as the Savior rather than the avenging Judge who will condemn guilty sinners to eternal hell. Those will be the only two ways to see God — Savior or Judge. We want to see Him as those who are blessed members of the kingdom. We want to behold Him in His beauty instead of His vengeance. So how can believers obediently pursue this purity of heart designed for true kingdom citizens?

Cultivating a Pure Heart

The Lord has transformed the heart of the believer; He has washed it clean. We must thoroughly examine ourselves for evidence of this internal transformation, but we must also simultaneously embark on an intentional cultivation of this purity. Here are eight areas with which to scrutinize the heart *and* foster its purity:

Prayer for God's Work

Ultimately, purity of heart is a work of God, and yet we are commanded to be pure. Since we cannot accomplish this precept apart from His supernatural power, we must pray for His Word to work in our hearts. The concept of us partnering with God in sanctification can quickly become misconstrued. Different approaches to sanctification have emerged as a consequence. Some wrongly conclude that since we've been washed clean, one must simply stand on that claim and believe it. The false doctrine of *perfectionism* teaches "a 'second blessing' of instant sanctification."[10] The problem is that sin still remains. This leads to a lack of guarding and a tendency to "follow the heart" which frequently ends in moral disaster. We must be alert to

---

10. R. C. Sproul, *Pleasing God: Discovering the Meaning and Importance of Sanctification* (Colorado Springs: David C Cook, 2012), 19.

the ongoing presence of sin in order to vigilantly protect and vigorously pursue holiness.

Undoubtedly, the phrase "let go, and let God" has ricocheted throughout mainstream Christianity. Also rooted in Keswick theology, this view of sanctification suggests that "faith is a force field against trouble, . . . a cause-and-effect kind of spirituality . . . more akin to the idea of karma."[11] It's all His work, and a Christian can do nothing apart from granting permission to God to operate, which in and of itself is grossly errant. Passively waiting will not produce holiness. We must partner with the Spirit in sanctification, just as Paul exhorted us to "cleanse ourselves from all defilement (2 Cor. 7:1). This means we are ardently striving for holiness while at the same time crying out to God in humble dependence for the power, desire, ability, and effectivity to actually reflect His purity. Our labor must begin with prayer.

After his sin with Bathsheba, David cried out, "Create in me a clean heart, O God, and renew a steadfast spirit within me" (Ps. 51:10). This was not a cry for salvation; rather, He pleaded with God to continue the work of purifying him because he knew God ultimately accomplished it—through our effort, but by His power. We see this duality in God's promise to believing Israel: "I will put My Spirit within you and cause you to walk in My statutes, and you will be careful to observe My ordinances" (Ezek. 36:27).

Remember that our formal and functional theology must align. While many readers may understand this truth, how well are you actually reflecting its reality through the quantity and quality of your prayers? Are you regularly and passionately praying to be conformed to the image of Christ? As sanctification is never completed in this life, so too should our prayers for it never cease. Any area where we are struggling with sin must be tracked back to our prayer lives. Are we

---

11. Jared C. Wilson, "The Devilishness of 'Let Go and Let God' Theology," The Gospel Coalition, November 20, 2019, https://www.thegospelcoalition.org.

recognizing our dependence on God to shape our very desires while we attend to our responsibility to combat sin with the resources He's already provided? Prayer is part of this intense exertion. It may sound passive, but we all know it can take incredible effort to pray well, particularly while the world, the flesh, and the devil constantly seek to distract and thwart us from this endeavor.

Devotion to the Truth

Next, we must possess a devotion to God's Word. Am I wowing you yet? Read your Bible and pray. While these disciplines may not sound innovative or cutting edge, they are the key to true change. Like prayer, how are we faring in our devotion to Scripture both in quantity and quality in our daily lives? If we want to effectively battle bitterness, resolve conflicts, break free from enslaving sin, and live lives pleasing to God, we need the Bible. We need to know, understand, desire, practice, and pray about Scripture. There's no mystical or mysterious way to living a life of purity, though it is undoubtedly supernatural.

God's Word is the source from which the truth necessary for purity flows; the Holy Spirit cleanses the heart through the Word as He illumines the principles of God's Word to empower purity. Knowing He accomplishes this, we must be utterly and desperately devoted to Scripture. Practical holiness is realized in our lives not by the Spirit zapping us, but as the principles are implemented. *We will never be holier than the degree to which we understand and apply Scripture.* It's that simple. If we know it, but fail to apply it, we will not be holy. The young man "keep[s] his way pure" by keeping God's Word (Ps. 119:9).

As discussed in chapter 5, we must fervently hunger for God's Word as "newborn babies long for the *pure* milk of the word, so that by it [we] may grow in respect to salvation" (1 Pet. 2:2). The benefits, blessings, and demonstration of our salvation all come from imbibing the Bible's pure words.

Certain movements in our society promote organic products, free from the synthetic and chemical substances and processes that the Industrial Age introduced. Many people expend much time and effort on researching and procuring the right kind of "pure" milk for their children, whether it's soy, oat, unpasteurized, coconut, cashew, skim, almond, or something else. Yet how much time do we spend consuming the Word's pure milk? There's nothing wrong with these other pursuits per se, unless we are failing to prioritize the most important kind of purity.

The pure words of Scripture will never fail to accomplish their purpose (Isa. 55:11). They are our very sustenance, and our lives should give abundant testimony to this fact. If not, we must set aside whatever is necessary in order to reflect it. The excuse of not having enough time falls flat throughout the corridors of human history. Never before have we had the basic needs of physical life met through such readily accessible conveniences. All of these technological blessings should lead us to a greater saturation of Scripture. If not, what might we need to remove from our lives? We can't afford to neglect the devotion to His pure words. David sang, "The words of the LORD are pure words; as silver tried in a furnace on the earth, refined seven times" (Ps. 12:6). They are wholly inerrant, infallible, and infinitely pure, reflecting God's own character. There is nothing in His Word that would detract from its value — not one speck of dross.

God's words are *pure* words. We hear and read so many words each day, whether it be from conversations, podcasts, movies and shows, books, social media, and more. Are they pouring forth *pure* words? Most likely not. In light of that, we would do better to listen a little more to the Word preached or read and a little less to our favorite commentator or influencer's hot take on the latest political narrative, streaming original, or social media trend. Imagine that instead of all those contaminated words from corrupt worldviews bouncing around in our minds, we were meditating on or memorizing biblical truth. We are shaped by what we take in; no matter how intelligent or impactful words from the world are, they can't offer what God's words offer:

> The law of the Lord is perfect, restoring the soul;
> The testimony of the Lord is sure, making wise the
> simple.
> The precepts of the Lord are right, rejoicing the heart;
> *The commandment of the Lord is pure, enlightening the*
> *eyes.* (Ps. 19:7-8, emphasis added)

If we want to be truly enlightened, to have our eyes opened so that we can perceive God rightly and ourselves clearly, we need the truth of God's Word. The foolish blindness and darkened ignorance of sin fall away as scales from our eyes. The Spirit works through the truths of Scripture to give us pure, unobstructed sight. When we see God clearly in all His glorious character, this drives our lives. It changes us when we gaze upon Christ: "But we all, with unveiled face, beholding as in a mirror the glory of the Lord, are being transformed into the same image from glory to glory, just as from the Lord, the Spirit" (2 Cor. 3:18).

David described the man of pure heart as "he who walks with integrity, and works righteousness, and speaks truth in his heart" (Ps. 15:2). We are constantly talking to ourselves in our inner man. In our hearts, so much of what we speak is untrue — about ourselves, others, and God. These thoughts, in turn, inform our attitudes and actions. *Holiness is predicated on truthful thinking.* We must tell ourselves true things based on Scripture's principles. David recognized that God "desire[d] truth in the innermost being, and in the hidden part" God would grant the wisdom needed to enable this right thinking (51:6). Our paramount priority must be to diligently seek after this God-given wisdom through Scripture as the only source to discover ultimate and unadulterated truth.

Exercise of Faith

After we focus on prayer and the Word, we then step forward to exercise faith. That is, we live according to the principles of the Word! It may not be easy, but it *is* simple. We are divinely convinced of the Bible's truths, and so we pursue them. Our remaining sin will fight our renewed heart, so we may not always want to obey. Our stubborn wills and affections are chafing against being driven by a love for God, but we still come underneath God's Word by the power of the Spirit who strengthens us. *That is faith in action.* It's how we both enter the kingdom and reside within it. In speaking of the salvation of the Gentiles to the Jewish Christians, Peter pointed out that God "made no distinction between [Jews and Gentiles], cleansing their hearts by faith" (Acts 15:9). Faith is the conduit through which purification comes. The Spirit of God produces it, and we must exercise it in our walk of sanctification. Paul reminded Timothy, "the goal of our instruction is love from a pure heart and a good conscience and a sincere faith" (1 Tim. 1:5).

Faith is like the scrub brush of the heart. Every time we exercise it, we are scrubbing away a little more sin. Every little scrub cleans and purifies a little more. Purity is not some giant spiritual project undertaken by a pious few aspiring to an upper echelon of Christian enlightenment. Simply showing up to church on Sunday morning to worship God is an exercise of faith that results in increased purity. That decision to not be bitter or angry when your child sins against you for the thousandth time; that honesty on your loan or job application when you know it may hurt your chances of acceptance; that consideration of your neighbor as more important than yourself, even though *your* interests are left unprotected and may be taken advantage of; that joyful contentment pursued in the midst of incredibly painful hardship and devastating loss—all these moments work together to scrub clean the dirty spots that remain in our inner man.

Or consider another illustration: Imagine you just inherited an old fixer-upper that desperately needs renovation. In fact, riddled with termite damage, the home is rotten to the core. So, you gut the entire interior, right down to the foundation. At that point, the building itself would be sound. It's been entirely renovated structurally, but that's it. The paint, for example, is still peeling and flaking, so you must scrape it off in order to reveal the newness underneath. Similarly, our hearts are transformed, but the crumbling paint of sin is still present. Every act of faith is another scrape, painfully scouring the sin to purify the renewed heart from the remaining corruption and corrosion.

Growth in the Fear of the Lord

Purity is always linked to a true fear of God. The fear of the Lord can be defined as *the delightful, dreadful, consuming, reverential awe of God that drives the lives and behavior of believers.* How truly weighty is God to us? To the extent that we properly perceive God in all His majestic glory we will pursue a heart of purity. In other words, *to the extent we fear God we will pursue holiness.*

Fearing God is the foundation for Christian living, the "beginning of wisdom" (Prov. 9:10). Fearing the Lord means that we rightly recognize Him as the great and mighty Savior "who loved [us] and gave Himself up for [us]" through His sacrificial death on the cross (Gal. 2:20). He must be weightier to us than other people, and yet so often we tend to fear man. *Any place that we fear man more than the Lord, we are unholy, and our purity is hindered.* When we allow our fear of others to drive our thinking and behavior, we idolatrously place them before God. This fear is rooted in a worry that people will not respond or relate to us in the manner we desire, revealing that we are actually worshipping ourselves. People-pleasing is really about self-pleasing. Every single thought, word, or action based on this fear is not holy. We must be driven by a biblical fear of God. God's expectations, desires, and concerns must be our own, not men's.

When we snuff out impurity in our lives, we are "perfecting holiness in the fear of God" (2 Cor. 7:1). Does this fear motivate everything we do as it should? Do we reflect often enough on the powerful character of God as the perfect, righteous Judge who promises to bring holy recompense for any due glory withheld from His creation? Do we frequently call to mind His awe-inspiring grace and mercy that suffered the penalty for our wicked rebellion in order to be eternally reconciled to Him? Why *shouldn't* this unfathomable Creator drive everything we do? Why would we ever let feeble, finite, foolish sinners utterly devoid of God's infinite mercy and grace determine what we do? Why would we allow our fleshly desires to drive us? What insanity! We must constantly remind ourselves of God's character and respond in trembling reverence in order to "make no provision for the flesh in regard to its lusts" (Rom. 13:14).

Maintaining a Clear Conscience

Next, we must maintain a clear conscience. Earlier in the chapter, we learned that our hearts have been cleansed from an evil conscience at conversion (Heb. 10:22). But rather than generating a passive acceptance, this actually means that believers now have a proper standard from which to calibrate our consciences. Before, when our consciences were tainted by our sinful nature, we could never properly understand the inner workings of the heart, so our own consciences were not always accurately condemning or approving. Believers, though, are enabled to inform their consciences with the principles of Scripture as illumined by the Spirit. This requires the continual transformation "by the renewing of [our] mind[s], so that [we] may prove what the will of God is, that which is good and acceptable and perfect" (Rom. 12:2). We need to be constantly growing in our understanding and applying that standard to our hearts. It is just as much work as it sounds. Moment-by-moment, we are examining and evaluating our thinking, desires, decisions, emotions, and all other heart activity.

The Bible states that the conscience bears witness by "alternately accusing or else defending" what our hearts produce (Rom. 2:15). Before a Roman governor and in reference to his ministry, Paul declared that he had done his "best to maintain always a blameless conscience both before God and before men" (Acts 24:16). Likewise, in everything we think, desire, feel, say, and do, we want our presiding consciences to be in accordance with God's Word: *Was that deed motivated by a love for God? Did my response help or hinder the hearer in his conformity to Christ's image?* Are we this intentional with our hearts on a daily basis? Do we know when we sin? Can we go to bed at the end of the day with a clear conscience? If we wait until bedtime, there's no way we can successfully recall the entire day's events and our heart's response at every moment. Instead, we have to be examining, thanking, confessing, and repenting throughout the entirety of the day. This is twenty-four-hour maintenance.

As you are reading this book right now, are you thinking about the thoughts going through your mind, deciding which can stay and which should be shown the exit? Does this sound exhausting yet? That's why we need the strength of God. It's why He dispenses His Spirit to indwell and empower us. We can't do it apart from Him; we would lose our minds trying. By His power and grace and because of the gospel, we can maintain a pure conscience. Paul gratefully attested that he had conducted himself based on "the testimony of [his] conscience, . . . in holiness and godly sincerity, not in fleshly wisdom but in the grace of God" (2 Cor. 1:12). We must follow suit.

Thinking on Pure Things

Imagine trying to keep a clean conscience while loading your mind with garbage. Straddling to embrace both the world and God will never yield purity. Feeding our hearts a steady diet of junk will seriously cripple our pursuit of holiness. We must fill our minds with the purity of truth. We must think rightly in every area of our lives. True thinking is pure thinking. We must be constantly screening everything that comes into our minds through the lens of Scripture. We're familiar with Paul's exhortation to the Philippians: "Finally, brethren, whatever is true, whatever is honorable, whatever is right, *whatever is pure*, whatever is lovely, whatever is of good repute, if there is any ex-cellence and if anything worthy of praise, dwell on these things" (Phil. 4:9, emphasis added). This applies to what comes *out* of the heart as well. This is a two-way gatekeeper, filtering out the impurities from both directions, since "the lust of the flesh and the lust of the eyes and the boastful pride of life" isn't just from our remaining sin, but "from the world" (1 John 2:16).

Thinking on "whatever is pure" does not mean that we can't consider the wrong in this world or avoid difficult matters. It simply means that we must appraise those issues accurately — that we under-stand them biblically, evaluating them properly according to God's Word. It's more than abstaining from profane movies, for example, but it's definitely not less than that. Our flesh loves feasting on junk; it may seem to taste good, but the more we grow in purity, the more we rightly discern what displeases the Lord and expel such impurity from our minds.

Intense Effort

Summing up the means of cultivating purity, its growth requires in-tense effort on our part. God's work is the central component even in our efforts. We partner with God, but that does not mean He meets us halfway as we each do our separate parts. Rather, our effort is one of the means by which God conforms us to Christ's character. Did you catch that subtle, but critical difference? God always uses means to accomplish His will, and our effort is really *His* work. That should bring both humility and comfort. He gets all of the credit because He is promoting and empowering our efforts, so He can use our striving to make us holy. Every part of our work is actually His supernatural work. This is how we walk by the Spirit so as not to "carry out the desires of the flesh" (Gal. 2:16).

With that in mind, we pray and exert tremendous effort to pur-sue righteousness. Paul instructed Timothy:

Therefore, if anyone cleanses himself from these things, he will be a vessel for honor, sanctified, useful to the Master, prepared for every good work. Now flee from youthful lusts and pursue righteousness, faith, love and peace, with those who call on the Lord from a pure heart. (2 Tim. 2:21–22)

Paul essentially commanded, "Flee! Run as fast as you can!" It takes energy and endurance to run from sin, along with training to do it well. Holiness does not crouch at the door (Gen. 4:7), lying in wait to overtake you. It's not lurking around the corner to fall upon you, though it would be nice if it did. That's what sin does. It's the sin "which so easily entangles us" (Heb. 12:1). We have to diligently pursue purity, because of the world, the flesh, and the devil waging war against our new, redeemed nature.

We must also remember that this is a team effort. We pursue holiness in the local church together as one body (Eph. 4:4). God has structured it to be done together. We don't have solo holiness that stands apart from the congregation. This means that we are dependent on one another. If someone is not pursuing holiness, the body is harmed and hampered in its growth along with the testimony of that church to the surrounding community. Those not actively pursuing holiness are hamstringing the rest of the congregation. *Any area we allow, confine, or harbor unholiness harms the entire effort of a church.* Let this motivate us to forsake sin and labor strenuously together.

The Reward

The Future Result

The corresponding reward for purity of heart is to see God. This is first and foremost a promise to behold Christ when He returns with actual sight—no longer by faith. Paul happily anticipated, "For now we see in a mirror dimly, but then face to face; now I know in part, but then I will know fully just as I also have been fully known (1 Cor. 13:12). We will survey Him in all His glory, but as we mentioned earlier, this sight will be different from the view of unbelievers:

> This is a plain indication of God's righteous judgment so that you will be considered worthy of the kingdom of God, for which indeed you are suffering. For after all it is only just for God to repay with affliction those who afflict you, and to give relief to you who are afflicted and to us as well when the Lord Jesus will be revealed from heaven with His mighty angels in flaming fire, dealing out retribution to those who do not know God and to those who do not obey the gospel of our Lord Jesus. These will pay the penalty of eternal destruction, away from the presence of the Lord and from the glory of His power, when He comes to be glorified in His saints on that day, and to be marveled at among all who have believed. (2 Thess. 1:5-10)

Paul comforted the Thessalonians with the hope that their suffering wasn't for naught, but that God would deal out judgment to their persecutors who didn't "obey the gospel of our Lord Jesus." The sight mentioned for faithful kingdom citizens will be to "marvel at" their glorified Lord and Savior in all His power. But the sight unbelievers will behold of the same Christ will be radically different. Their wrathful Judge will be "revealed from heaven with His mighty angels in flaming fire." What's more, after their judgment, their sight of the risen Christ will abruptly come to an immediate end. They will see Him, and then they will never be allowed to behold Him ever again for all eternity. Kingdom citizens, however, will forever gaze on Him in all His magnificent splendor, knowing and worshiping Him. Does purity of heart sound worth it? It is. In anticipation of this future sight, we must pursue holiness "without which no one will see the Lord" (Heb. 12:14).

The Present Result

When we seek purity of heart, we will manifest the fruit of the Spirit that are promised in Scripture. Since we have "purified [our] souls for a sincere love of the brethren," we will "fervently love one another from the heart" (1 Pet. 1:22). With our purified conscience, we will be devoted to "prayers night and day" (2 Tim. 1:3). We will proclaim the gospel "from pure motives" and care for the afflicted as we "keep [ourselves] unstained by the world" (Phil. 1:17; James 1:27). We will exercise godly wisdom that "is first pure, then peaceable, gentle, reasonable, full of mercy and good fruits, unwavering, without hypocrisy" (James 3:17). We will enjoy "ascend[ing] into the hill of the LORD" through fellowship with Him as those who have "clean hands and a pure heart" (Ps. 24:3–4).

When we as a church pursue purity, we are also becoming a suitable bride for Christ. Paul shared that he had "betrothed [the Corinthian church] to one husband," so that he could present them "as a pure virgin" (2 Cor. 11:2). But he warned them that if they chase after impurity, their "minds [would] be led astray from the simplicity and purity of devotion to Christ" (11:3). The Holy Spirit is progressively fitting us for this marriage that will be consummated when Christ returns. Is our Groom our paramount passion? He must be, and our purity confirms and reinforces it. Just as lustfulness, pornography, and adultery destroy the sacred marital bond a couple shares, so impurity of heart rips us away from esteeming Christ's weightiness and enjoying His presence. In light of all of this, let us arduously scrub our hearts clean in preparation for eternity with our King.

~

Blest are the pure, whose hearts are clean
from the defiling pow'rs of sin;
with endless pleasure they shall see
a God of spotless purity.

~Isaac Watts, 1709

Questions for Reflection & Discussion

1. Define *purity of heart.*

2. How are believers able to actually be holy?

3. Why were the Pharisees hypocritical? How is purity of heart the opposite of this? Which is your heart primarily characterized by?

4. Explain indwelling sin in the believer's heart using the illustration from the chapter.

5. What are some practical ways to guard our hearts from the internal sin? And from external influences?

6. How regularly do you pray for your sanctification (and others in the body)? What's the relationship between our partnership with God in sanctification?

7. Do our lives "give abundant testimony" that Scripture is our very sustenance? Why or why not? If not, what do we need to remove?

8. Describe the process of biblical change. What is the role of faith?

9. Define the fear of the Lord. Is God weighty to you? In what situations do you tend to fear man over God? What's one practical step you can take this week to overcome your fear of man (i.e., people-pleasing)?

10. Do you evaluate your thinking? Do you measure your thoughts against Scripture? Why is that so important? How can you start or improve?

11. What's your reward for pursuing purity of heart? Does this appeal to you? Does it sound worth it?

12. Where are there impurities in your heart that you need to deal with? What's the first actionable step to burning those impurities away?

Chapter 8

Blessed Are the Peacemakers

Blessed are the peacemakers, for they shall be
called sons of God.

Remarking on the bloody track record European nations'
shared with one another, someone cynically observed:
"What they call peace is the little time necessarily spent in
reloading their guns."[1] Time has certainly confirmed the veracity of
this witticism penned in the late 1800s. But popular opinion at that
time began gravitating toward predictions of world peace. The scientific discoveries and technological innovations of human progress would usher in a new age, they claimed, where war was irrational and contrary to national interests. Countries, it was argued,
were "too economically interdependent to make war between them

---

1. Robert G. Ingersoll, "Reply to the Indianapolis Clergy," *The Works of Robert G. Ingersoll* (New York: C.P. Farrell, 1900), 7:139.

a profitable exercise."[2] This triumph was declared just three years prior to World War I, the so-called "war to end all wars," breaking out across the globe and resulting in millions dead.[3] Yet hope in human nature rebounded undeterred, as "peace for our time" was infamously proclaimed less than a year before World War II.[4]

The reason war has never ceased on our planet is because human nature is fundamentally not at peace. Because of our fallenness, humanity can't get along with one another. We demand other individuals or groups defer to our own interests and ideas. That's who we are at the core. But ultimately, we are not at peace with our Maker. He is warring against mankind due to their rebellious sinfulness. This is shocking to the man on the street. *Sure, men fight each other, but God is at peace with all of us,* he might conclude to himself. *If we could just remember we are all His children, we could get along and everything would be fine.* But God is not fine with us as we are because He wars against sin. The Bible is clear that "the wrath of God is revealed from heaven against all ungodliness and unrighteousness of men who suppress the truth in unrighteousness," which is man's natural condition and primary problem in life (Rom. 1:18). As a result, mankind can never have peace with one another until we first have peace with God:

> With all of the avowed and well-intentioned efforts for peace in modern times, few people would claim that the world or any significant part of it is more peaceful now than a hundred years ago. We do not have economic peace, religious peace, racial peace, social peace, family peace, or personal peace. There seems to be no end of marches, sit-ins, rallies, protests, demonstrations, riots, and wars. Disagreement

---

2. Michael Rühle, "The End of the 'Great Illusion': Norman Angell and the Founding of NATO, *NATO Review*, January 14, 2019, https://www.nato.int.
3. H. G. Wells, *The War That Will End War* (Redditch, UK: Read Books Ltd., 2016).
4. Neville Chamberlain, "Peace For Our Time" (speech), 10 Downing St., London, September 30, 1938, https://eudocs.lib.byu.edu.

and conflict are the order of the day. No day has had more need of peace than our own.[5]

The world will be in need of peace every day until Christ returns. We need peace with God in order to live in harmony with Him *and* peace with fellow believers to live in harmony with His people. As we practice peace within God's family, we credibly demonstrate the gift of God's peace to a dying world around us. When there is no peace in the church, however, there will be little effective work for Christ. The peace offered by the church to unbelievers will not be perceived as precious or even desirable if the visible body is not at peace with one another.

True kingdom living is evidenced by both a continual pursuit of peace within the church and a passionate proclamation of peace to the culture. The world is incapable of maintaining peace, but the church can and must. Christ's bride must not war amongst herself.

As we approach the end of the beatitudes, their progression should be evident. There is no way to be a peacemaker unless we have first been poor in spirit, contrite over our sin, gently submissive to God, longing for His holiness, and practicing it through compassion for others and purity of heart. As we noted, these heart attitudes work their way toward outward expression—first within the church, and then directed outward to the unbelieving world. We are thoroughly preparing ourselves for the persecution coming in the last beatitude as we cultivate the character needed to endure it.

Peace will always be a strenuous, ongoing effort. If there is even one point of conflict in our churches, families, or lives that hasn't been resolved, we must continue to strive for reconciliation. Because of our remaining sin, multidimensional points for conflict abound in every single relationship. Kingdom citizens have much work to do. We can

---

5. John MacArthur, *Matthew 1–7*, vol. 1, *The MacArthur New Testament Commentary* (Chicago: Moody Press, 1985), 210.

start by understanding what Jesus meant when He said, "Blessed are the peacemakers."

Defining a Peacemaker

There are many words for *peace* in Scripture. It's referenced hundreds of times, but this is the only place in the entire New Testament that this particular Greek word for *peacemaker* is used. The term carries the connotation of a mediator, someone who seeks to bring a harmonious relationship between two opposing parties. Similar to the heart of mercy, the idea is more than just desiring peace, or even being at peace; it's a longing for others to be at peace that drives us to diligently labor to that end. *A biblical peacemaker, therefore, is one who delights in exerting maximum effort to bring reconciliation between opposing parties as a demonstration of the character and work of God.* True believers rejoice in this arduous ministry, resting in the knowledge that it is God who ultimately allows peace to be made. His power and work are behind our efforts.

Reconciliation is a theological term that describes a restoration of relationship between two parties who are at odds, or at least one with the other. Again, this horizontal peacemaking between men cannot be accomplished before the vertical reconciliation between God and man has been established. Both acts are the direct expression of God's nature. He is the great Peacemaker. He is the One whose heart independently longs for peace and works to see it brought to fruition. He graciously implants both the desire and the ability within us; otherwise, we would be neck-deep in conflict, warring to protect our own interests and fundamentally incapable of making true peace with anyone. God commands believers to pursue peace. With indwelling sin remaining, peace is continually fleeing from us; we must always be actively pursuing and maintaining it as God commands.

The Necessity of Peacemaking

Necessary for Kingdom Entrance

Before we go any further, we need to lay the foundation upon which our peacemaking toward others is built—that is, God's peacemaking toward us. Remember that each of these characteristics in the Beatitudes reflects the heart change necessary to gain admission into the kingdom. Scripture is clear that we all, apart from Christ, are "haters of God," sinful, and at war with Him (Rom. 1:30). Romans explicitly states that man is "hostile toward God;" he refuses to subject himself to God's law, is incapable of obedience in the first place, and fundamentally cannot please Him (Rom. 8:7–8). In fact, His transcendent holiness demands not only a hatred of sin, but justice. John the Baptist clearly warned, "He who believes in the Son has eternal life; but he who does not obey the Son will not see life, but the wrath of God abides on him" (John 3:36). Paul explained that "the wrath of God is revealed from heaven against all ungodliness and unrighteousness of men who suppress the truth in unrighteousness" (Rom. 1:18). While worldly conventional wisdom envisions an amicable God who's peaceful toward all, the Bible reveals that this righteous Creator is actively warring against humanity's sin.

For there to be peace there must be pain and difficulty because we inherited a sinful nature. We enter the world tainted and broken. This is why the One who came to bring peace first stated, "Do not think that I came to bring peace on the earth; I did not come to bring peace, but a sword" (Matt. 10:34). Just as with two warring nations, conflict occurs before peace is achieved. Christ wields the sword of God's Word to expose our sin and testify to God's wrath against mankind. This painful blow that "pierc[es] as far as the division of soul and spirit, of both joints and marrow, and [is] able to judge the thoughts and intentions of the heart" generates the proper mourning and spiritual bankruptcy from which a "broken and a contrite" spirit emerges (Heb. 4:12; Ps. 51:17). We've witnessed this progression in the Beatitudes themselves as it pertains to entrance into the kingdom:

> Until unrighteousness is changed to righteousness there cannot be godly peace. And the process of resolution is difficult and costly. Truth will produce anger before it produces happiness; righteousness will produce antagonism before it produces harmony. The gospel brings bad feelings before it can bring good feelings. A person who does not first mourn over his own sin will never be satisfied with God's righteousness. The sword that Christ brings is the sword of His Word which is the sword of truth and righteousness. Like the surgeon's scalpel, it must cut before it heals, because peace cannot come where sin remains.[6]

We have no doubt experienced this in our evangelistic efforts. When we proclaim to men their sinfulness and God's righteous wrath against them, rarely do they agree and rejoice. Typically, they feel greatly offended, unfairly judged, and desirous to get away. But the good news of God providing a way through Christ for reconciliation makes no sense unless we first realize we are His enemies. Real, lasting peace *can* be achieved in our lifetime according to His great mercy and grace displayed in the gospel message. He is the sole Peacemaker, "in that while we were yet sinners, Christ died for us" (Rom. 5:8). In our sin, we didn't long for peace; we would have stayed at war, "dead in [our] trespasses and sins, . . . by nature children of wrath, even as the rest" (Eph. 2:1; 3). God must first move — what a blessing He did and at such a dear cost to Himself! His righteous wrath and holy justice converged with His loving grace and merciful forgiveness on the cross through the work of Jesus Christ.

---

6. MacArthur, *Matthew* (1985), 211–212.

God's wrath has been fully satisfied for those who repent and believe in His Son; the righteous anger has been entirely placated. Christ was our peace offering, our propitiatory sacrifice. The enmity is gone, but we are not left merely in a state of ceased hostility. In imputing Christ's righteousness to us, we are placed into union with Him and enabled to have a harmonious, loving relationship with God. Romans concludes, "Therefore, having been justified by faith, we have peace with God through our Lord Jesus Christ, through whom also we have obtained our introduction by faith into this grace in which we stand" (Rom. 5:1). Our salvation allows us to enter into peaceful relations with God through repentance and faith.

The gospel message also enables men to have true peace with one another based on their unity in Christ as new citizens of the same kingdom. Referencing the former division between Jews and Gentiles, Paul observed of the New Covenant:

> But now in Christ Jesus you who formerly were far off have been brought near by the blood of Christ. For He Himself is our peace, who made both groups into one and broke down the barrier of the dividing wall, by abolishing in His flesh the enmity, which is the Law of commandments contained in ordinances, so that in Himself He might make the two into one new man, thus establishing peace, and might reconcile them both in one body to God through the cross, by it having put to death the enmity. And He came and preached peace to you who were far away, and peace to those who were near; for through Him we both have our access in one Spirit to the Father. So then you are no longer strangers and aliens, but you are fellow citizens with the saints, and are of God's household, having been built on the foundation of the apostles and prophets, Christ Jesus Himself being the corner stone, in whom the whole building,

being fitted together, is growing into a holy temple in the Lord, in whom you also are being built together into a dwelling of God in the Spirit. (Eph. 2:13–22)

United by Christ's work and the indwelling of the Holy Spirit, we have each been given a new identity in Him that supersedes every other identity. We are all members now of the same body with "no distinction between Greek and Jew, circumcised and uncircumcised, barbarian, Scythian, slave and freeman" (Col. 3:11). Christ brings believers together.

But there is yet another peace. Believers are commissioned to take the saving message of the gospel to unbelievers so that they may hear, repent, believe, and also gain admittance into the kingdom. God has chosen to accomplish this by tasking the church with the mission. God saves people as they hear the good news proclaimed by His people. It's imperative we do not neglect this responsibility. People must have the path to peace communicated to them: "How then will they call on Him in whom they have not believed? How will they believe in Him whom they have not heard? And how will they hear without a preacher?" (Rom. 10:14) We must be faithful to proclaim the gospel, "for it is the power of God for salvation to everyone who believes" (1:16). Once we are saved by His grace, God graciously gives us the opportunity to take part in His work to reconcile others to Himself:

Now all these things are from God, who reconciled us to Himself through Christ and gave us the ministry of reconciliation, namely, that God was in Christ reconciling the world to Himself, not counting their trespasses against them, and He has committed to us the word of reconciliation. Therefore, we are ambassadors for Christ, as though God were making an appeal through us; we beg you on behalf of Christ, be reconciled to God. He made Him who knew no sin to be sin on our behalf, so that we might become the righteousness of God in Him. (2 Cor. 5:19–21)

What an exciting message we have to proclaim! No wonder Isaiah rejoiced:

How lovely on the mountains
Are the feet of him who brings good news,
Who announces peace
And brings good news of happiness (Isa. 52:7)

As God's emissaries, we humbly serve as little peacemakers. We don't forge the peace, but we point to the God who has. Perhaps you share your testimony with an agnostic coworker or your rebellious child; participate in your church's street evangelism or pass out neighborhood flyers for Vacation Bible School; help plant a church in a nation with marginal evangelical presence or fund a Bible translation for an isolated people group. The church is busy about God's business of proclaiming the peace that purchased and provided entrance into His kingdom.

Necessary for Kingdom Living

We have discussed God's vertical peace toward those who repent and believe, the reality of horizontal peace among fellow believers, and our proclamation of God's peace to unbelievers. These are all intertwined. D.A. Carson observes,

Jesus does not limit the peacemaking to only one kind, and neither will his disciples. In the light of the gospel, Jesus himself is the supreme peacemaker, making peace between God and man, and man and man. Our peacemaking . . . must also extend to seeking all kinds of reconciliation. Instead of delighting in division, bitterness, strife, or some petty "divide-

and-conquer" mentality, disciples of Jesus delight to make peace wherever possible. Making peace is not appeasement: the true model is God's costly peace-making.[7]

As God draws sinners into the fold, we must constantly be working at living harmoniously with fellow kingdom citizens who "are of God's household" (Eph. 2:19). Our own relationships are the primary witness testifying to the transforming power of the gospel to the outside watching world.

It seems logical to expect that redeemed people would easily get along—God, who gave all of us His Spirit, placed us together in the same condition as new creatures united in Christ. Shouldn't perfect harmony be an effortless foregone conclusion? While the foundation for peace with one another has been laid through God's work, we still have indwelling sin that obstructs and mars our relations. As Scripture commands, then, we must be "diligent to preserve the unity of the Spirit in the bond of peace" (Eph. 4:3). Because we are sinful, we must continually work to foster peace, which is necessary to maintain unity. *Only when and until peace is pursued can the church serve as peacemakers to the dying world around us.* It is critical that we fulfill this role within the church so that we can effectively fulfill the Great Commission. Otherwise, our evangelistic efforts are hindered: why would an unbeliever have reason to believe our message of peace with God if we can't even achieve peace within the church? How credible is that testimony? When the peace of the church is strong, her evangelism is strong; but when the peace of the church is weak, her evangelism is likewise weak. Our light is dimmed, so we must continuously strive for peace within the church. This pleases the Lord and glorifies His name by reflecting His greatness.

---

7. D. A. Carson, *The Expositor's Bible Commentary*, eds. Tremper Longman III and David E. Garland, vol. 9, *Matthew ~ Mark*, (Grand Rapids: Zondervan, 2010), 135.

In fact, living out the role of peacemaker within the kingdom demonstrates the reality that we are indeed "sons of God" as the beatitude promises. God's children are characterized by peacemaking. A church member cannot both claim kingdom citizenship and yet be at constant war with His people. If he contentiously refuses to resolve conflict and forgive sin, he is either a disobedient believer forfeiting his assurance by enslavement to deeply rooted sin, or he is not truly a child of God at all: "Peacemaking is a hallmark of God's children. . . . The person who is continually disruptive, divisive, and quarrelsome has good reason to doubt his relationship to God altogether."[8]

However, this does not mean peacemaking is easy. There are many challenges that can threaten peace in the body, not the least of which are issues of the conscience. Romans 14–15 addresses peacekeeping within this context after Paul already dealt with theological matters in the first eleven chapters. Those fundamental truths, particularly on the nature of salvation, cannot brook differing views, but Paul transitioned into the realm of personal liberty. Just as believers who emerged from Judaism in his day wrestled with religious observances and dietary regulations, so too believers in our contemporary society grapple with positions on various issues for which the Bible grants freedom. Paul explained:

> For he who in this way serves Christ is acceptable to God and approved by men. So then we pursue the things which make for peace and the building up of one another. Do not tear down the work of God for the sake of food. All things indeed are clean, but they are evil for the man who eats and gives offense. It is good not to eat meat or to drink wine, or to do anything by which your brother stumbles. (Rom. 14:18–21)

8. MacArthur, *Matthew* (1985), 217–218.

The proclivity for humanity to desire reference points by which to measure abstract or subjective qualities transcends both time and culture. We want to quantify and compare ourselves, and we do it just as much today as they did back then. We may not cover our faces in ash and announce to the world we are fasting beyond the law's requirements like the Pharisees, but we have our own ways of gauging spiritual maturity. This danger can breed legalism and be a source of divisive unrest. Paul pointed out that in passing judgment on those topics for which even God gives license, we place ourselves above His own impeccable standard of judgment. What sinful arrogance! Within church circles, there are some common areas where seeds of discord may frequently be sown:

- *Media content*: While some content is explicitly evil, there are many approaches for how to use technology, which technologies, when, how often, in what context, based on what age, and so much more—levels of violence in video games; time spent scrolling, swiping, or surfing; political debate amidst tweets and posts; movies with worldly messages; lyrics of popular songs; ages for children to have a smartphone; fantasy or romance books; online dating; and the list could easily continue. While personal convictions or family positions informed by biblical principles can be helpful to navigate these kinds of decisions, they cannot be used as a litmus test by which to judge others' assessments or even spirituality.

- *Education*: Whether other parents in the church choose to home-school or send their children to public or private schools, their decision is not necessarily a reflection of their spiritual status. No one is holier in God's eyes because their children are home-schooled; it is a secondary conscience issue for which parents must be afforded leeway. To be sure, heart motives can render an inherently amoral decision sinful, but as long as they are pursuing their decision in a godly way and not violating any biblical principles, they are free to choose. This applies to schooling techniques as well, and yet bitter rifts have harmed relationships within churches over differing views on these matters.

- *Diet*: We have brought "clean" and "unclean" foods back into style according to our own determinations. Based on health considerations, that's not innately wrong unless we attach spiritual value to them or judge others who don't conform to our evaluations. If we are firmly convinced that only non-GMO, organic, unprocessed, gluten-free foods are safe and healthy to consume, we are tempted to assume the woman who feeds her children fast food hates her family and presumes on God's grace. This can go the other direction as well, though. As a fan and former employee of my favorite fast-food chain, I must remember that I am not holier simply because *my* moral scruples freely welcome Big Macs, nor should I flaunt it.

- *Other issues*: Drinking, co-ed swimming, appearance (hairstyles, modesty parameters, etc.), secular holiday traditions, political affiliations, vaccinations, the nature and content of leisure time, and a host of other areas. We all have varying stances and opinions on these concerns, so we must learn to live with one another peacefully.

Paul instructed, "If possible, so far as it depends on you, be at peace with all men" (Rom. 12:18). While his command is in the context of relations with those outside the church, we can do no less within the body.

Pursuing peace also goes hand-in-hand with our pursuit of holiness and truth: "Pursue peace with all men, and the sanctification without which no one will see the Lord" (Heb. 12:14). If we are not growing in godliness, we cannot grow in our peacemaking efforts. Comforting persecuted believers who were eagerly looking to Christ's return, Peter wrote, "Therefore, beloved, since you look for these things, be diligent to be found by Him in peace, spotless and blameless" (2 Pet. 3:14). Peace is a fruit of the Spirit that we grow in as we pursue our sanctification. If Christ returned at this very moment, would we be found "in peace"? Would we be found as having been diligent to resolve every conflict in our lives with other believers? God uses the church through His Word to dispense every tool and resource we need to resolve conflicts with other Christians, so we are without excuse. This may include approaching church leadership or a godly mediator within the church to help because these conflicts *must* be resolved. Every effort must be made because it is that crucial.

The Practice of Peacemaking

What can we practically pursue to develop our peacemaking character as believers? Let's examine several principles that will help us fulfill this role to which we have been called by God.

Exercise Love

We must lay the foundation with love—deep, practical, relational love. If we don't possess love, we will never solve any conflict. Scripture affirms anything accomplished apart from a motivation of love "profits [us] nothing" (1 Cor. 13:3). In fact, not only are our works meaningless, but *we* are also nothing without love (v. 2). This means that our spiritual footprint is non-existent if we are devoid of love. The essence of a believer, like God, is to love:

> God's people are to contend without being contentious, to disagree without being disagreeable, and to confront without being abusive. The peacemaker

speaks the truth in love (Eph. 4:15). To start with love is to start towards peace.[9]

Love does not "rejoice in unrighteousness" (1 Cor. 13:6), so peace does not overlook sin by saying that it doesn't matter, even when we may choose to cover offenses for some time (1 Pet. 4:8). Love confronts ongoing sin issues, but it always does so in a gracious, humble manner. *True, biblical love is a desire above all things to see others conformed to the image of Christ.* When believers may wrestle and grow weary, love steps in to "admonish the unruly, encourage the fainthearted, help the weak, [and] be patient with everyone" (1 Thess. 5:14). Love is full-orbed. It pursues Christ-conformity through the gracious exercise of all Christian virtues so that God receives maximum glory. Without it, peacemaking will become either bitter and contentious on the one hand, or weak and spineless on the other.

Finally, exercising this kind of love must start in the home with spouses and children who profess Christ. We must remember they represent the church as well. The pursuit of peacemaking within the local body will mean very little if we're continually at odds with members of our own household. The other principles in this list must all begin in the home as well.

Love Righteousness

Next, we must sincerely love righteousness. As just mentioned, godliness and peace are directly connected. If we fail to passionately pursue righteousness, we will be ineffective peacemakers. In describing godly wisdom, James said it's first "pure, then peaceable" (James 3:17). Because of our devotion to holiness, we will expend every resource to seek peace. This kind of heart longs to be in harmony with fellow believers and will bring biblical principles to bear in order to resolve

---

9. MacArthur, *Matthew* (1985), 217.

any obstacle to peace. Our dedication to purity flows out in peace. James continued to describe wisdom as "gentle, reasonable, full of mercy and good fruits, unwavering, without hypocrisy" (v. 17). James heavily borrowed from the Sermon on the Mount for his epistle. This passage is quite reminiscent of the Beatitudes, which is why we have cited it for the third time in this book. Jesus' brother continued, "And the seed whose fruit is righteousness is sown in peace by those who make peace" (v. 18). The order is reversed; peace sown reaps righteousness and righteousness sown reaps more peace. This should be the church — a continual harvest of righteousness and peace. Conflicts begin to disappear as soon as they pop up because they are being resolved. We diligently deal with each of them day by day, swiftly and diligently, so we have resources to invest in the new ones that will inevitably arise due to our indwelling sin.

By no means, however, do we sacrifice truth on the altar of peace; they do not have an inverse relationship. Peace cannot be pursued at the expense of righteous truth. Rather, it is achieved through it. To reiterate from chapter 5, *holiness solves everything*. Two believers cannot be at peace until they recognize and repent from any wrong attitudes, motivations, or actions that caused the conflict between them in the first place. Any other peace that fails to deal with sin is neither righteous nor durable. It is merely a veneer underneath which a cold, selfish vindictiveness lurks. It manipulates, plays a part, and finally closes the heart and avoids the other person altogether. The less righteous we are, the more selfish and less peaceable we will be. We tolerate peace as long as everyone around us agrees with what we want. When each of us pursues our own selfish desires, conflict is inescapable. The church declares war against herself. When we love righteousness, only then will peace actually grow.

Abhor Selfishness

Selfishness chafes against peacemaking. In our text from James, he was describing godly wisdom in contrast to human wisdom. Deferring to our own judgment is "not that which comes down from above, but is earthly, natural, demonic, for where jealousy and selfish ambition exist, there is disorder and every evil thing" (vv. 15–16). When I see a church, relationship, or marriage wracked with discord, I know jealousy and selfish ambition are not far. Selfishness declares, *I will get what I want, and if I don't, I'll blame you.* It will be primarily expressed through the broad spectrum of sinful anger and will fan the flames of dissension and discontentment. Jealousy grumbles, *I don't just deserve what others have; I don't want them to have what they have.* It constantly bemoans, *Why do they get that nice house? Why is their family that perfect? Why does he get to have that giftedness? Why does everyone want to be his friend?* This is evil. It's earthly, natural, and demonic, as James revealed, and it ravages peace. Our selfishness inhibits peace with others, and we must learn to hate it.

We must cultivate instead a self-denial that seeks to serve others before ourselves. Paul commanded us to "not just please ourselves" (Rom. 15:1), but "to please [our] neighbor for his good, to his edification" (v. 2). While this is in the context of brethren with both stronger and weaker consciences, the principle of "regard[ing] one another as more important than [ourselves]" still applies (Phil. 2:3). What would our churches look like if one of our primary concerns was ensuring that others were being uplifted and edified? What if we were motivated to avoid conflict simply because it would tear others down and fail to benefit them? Christ possessed this selfless character, as "even [He] did not please Himself" (Rom. 5:3). In fact, He was our perfect example to have "this attitude in [ourselves]" (Phil. 2:5).

In order to grow in selflessness, we must actively despise selfishness. We need to accurately perceive it in all its ugliness—as oozing slime that seeps out of the corners of our hearts from the wicked flesh that remains. It's heinous, odious, and grotesque. It causes division and isn't welcome in God's kingdom. It must be banished and exiled from our lives. We replace it with "righteousness and peace and joy in the Holy Spirit" (Rom. 14:17). Since this transformation is carried out by the Spirit's power, we know that only believers have the ability to do this. The fact that many times we squander the resources the Spirit provides is more shameful than unbelievers being unable to demonstrate true selflessness. Thankfully God never commands us without also supplying the power with which to obey. By implication, there is no conflict too great that can't find a biblical resolution that pleases God. He always provides abundant power for that which He commands.

Be Accepting

Paul continued in Romans 15,

> Now may the God who gives perseverance and encouragement grant you to be of the same mind with one another according to Christ Jesus, so that with one accord you may with one voice glorify the God and Father of our Lord Jesus Christ (vv. 5–6).

Unity is our goal. To accomplish this aim, the apostle commanded, "Therefore, accept one another, just as Christ also accepted us to the glory of God" (v. 7). This acceptance is a faithful commitment. It says, *I'm going to accept you when you wrestle and when you rub me the wrong way because I care for you.* This doesn't mean accepting sin as already mentioned. Spurgeon clarified: "Our peaceableness is never to be a compact with sin, or toleration of evil. We must set our faces like flints against everything which is contrary to God and his holiness."[10] But it does mean never giving up on other believers, helping them in their struggles, and always looking for ways to draw them into a deeper relationship.

Sadly, many times we act like immature kids on the playground instead. We enjoy our exclusive cliques that are constantly being redefined in terms of who's in and who's out. If someone does something

---

10. Charles Spurgeon, *Evening by Evening* (New York: Sheldon & Co., 1869), 77.

we don't like, we push them out of our circles. It's unfortunate on the playground, but it's even more tragic among believing adults. We just get subtler and more sophisticated in our approach. We stiff-arm people and look for excuses to keep them at arm's length. Someone offends us, inadvertently or otherwise, and we slice off a little sliver of peace with that fellow believer along with a bitterness that stands ready to carve off more. Imagine the entire congregation engaging in such detrimental behavior and in short order, that church is a mangled mess. Instead, we must eagerly find ways to welcome, include, and pull people into our spheres, pursuing peace with them at every turn. Again, we don't accept sin, nor do we overlook erroneous doctrine, but even in those most difficult areas, we work through those issues in every way possible and appropriate to maintain peace.

Cultivate Like-mindedness

Even though we accept others and respect their consciences in the myriad areas where differences can pose a threat to peace, we must also simultaneously strive for like-mindedness within the body. We embrace everyone right where they are, biblically-speaking, but the goal is to grow together in unity. We are all progressing toward conformity to the same image—Christ's. Paul instructed the church at Corinth to "be like-minded, live in peace; and the God of love and peace will be with you" (2 Cor. 13:11).

He likewise charged the Philippians to "make [his] joy complete by being of the same mind, maintaining the same love, united in spirit, intent on one purpose" (Phil. 2:2). The Greek term for "united in spirit" literally translates as "fellow-souled."[11] Further down in the letter, he referred to Timothy as a "kindred spirit" (v. 20); broken down, *isopsychos* translates as "equal-souled."[12] The mandate for biblical unity

---

11. W. E. Vine, *Vine's Complete Expository Dictionary of Old and New Testament Words*, vol. 1 (Nashville: Thomas Nelson, 1996), 23.
12. Vine, *Dictionary*, vol. 2 (1996), 343.

is not a potential threat to peace, but a means by which to achieve it. Our united purpose is to glorify God through looking like Jesus together, not to exalt our differences over one another. When this mission is at the forefront, conflicts get resolved. The church that longs to look like Jesus overcomes her differences and maintains peace.

Stop Grumbling

Remaining in Philippians 2, we find that Paul gave another practical command for maintaining peace in the church. Resonating with the epistle's overarching theme of joyful unity in the body of Christ, the apostle urged, "Do all things without grumbling or disputing" (v. 14). This is so much more than a verse for moms to rattle off when their children resist taking out the garbage, although that is certainly a fitting application. The primary context pertains to maintaining that like-mindedness with one another. He revealed the motivation in the following verse: "So that you will prove yourselves to be blameless and innocent, children of God above reproach in the midst of a crooked and perverse generation, among whom you appear as lights in the world" (v. 15). Grumbling against the leadership and one another in the body sows seeds of discord. It is never appropriate. Legitimate grievances should be properly addressed by dealing directly with involved parties, not by covertly complaining to others.

Paul had in mind the Israelites who wandered in the desert before entering the promised land of Canaan. They were continually grumbling against God, Moses, and one another, and God judged them for it. When believers withhold complaint, the world sees God's character. They recognize the stark contrast since the world is characterized by a complaining nature. If you work with unbelievers, you have undoubtedly noticed this difference. They have grumbling spirits against the supervisors, employers, company policies, fellow coworkers, compensation, and customers; and in between work complaints, they personally air their grievances over the government, their kids, the weather, their in-laws, their neighbors, their spouse, and everything and everybody else. It is crucial that the church be different. Real issues may arise within the church, but we need to work to resolve them according to biblical principles that are saturated in love for both God and fellow kingdom citizens. Resolution may only be able to go so far, and that's all that can be done. If the church is sound with qualified leadership, we can joyfully submit and drop the matter if necessary. When we share it with others not directly involved, we are killing the church by disrupting her peace.

Extend Forgiveness

Kingdom citizens may also practice peacemaking by always extending forgiveness when they are the offended party. In laying aside the old nature, we are told to "let all bitterness and wrath and anger and clamor and slander be put away from [us], along with all malice" (Eph. 4:31). If we fully forgive, none of the listed sins should be our response. These transgressions of the tongue are deadly to peace. Rather than launching a direct assault, however, we may subtly injure the offender through purposely sharing "dainty morsels" of gossip about our him (Prov. 18:8). In conversation with others, we can even convey our resentment with a raising of the eyebrows or knowing sigh when the offender is mentioned. Even a vague reference to him needing prayer can be a means by which we exact revenge.

Instead, we should instantly forgive our fellow believers, so the offenses disappear. There may be certain aspects or consequences that must be worked through, heavily at times and involving relevant parties, but the pardon is freely and instantly granted.[13] We should no longer be tempted to speak poorly of our offenders because the offense has already been dealt with—it was forgiven. There's nothing on which to dwell, no record of wrongs on which to keep score, no bit-

---

13. Sadly, there are a number of sins so grievous they may need to involve the authorities and possibly criminal punishment. Even in these instances, heartfelt forgiveness is still possible in Christ, as well as biblical love that seeks the offender's highest good—repentance and Christlikeness.

terness to harbor, no justice to exact, and nothing to share. This kind of genuine, biblical forgiveness is only possible because of Christ's person and work. We are enabled to forgive much because *we've* been forgiven much. Furthermore, Christ has already paid the penalty for the sins of fellow believers. If God's wrath has already been satisfied regarding the offense, we are empowered to forgive and forget freely.

Refuse Revenge

Resisting the temptation to seek satisfaction for wrongs against us is an extension of the forgiveness just discussed. Paul took the Roman church through this process:

> If possible, so far as it depends on you, be at peace with all men. Never take your own revenge, beloved, but leave room for the wrath of God, for it is written, "VENGEANCE IS MINE, I WILL REPAY," says the Lord. "BUT IF YOUR ENEMY IS HUNGRY, FEED HIM, AND IF HE IS THIRSTY, GIVE HIM A DRINK; FOR IN SO DOING YOU WILL HEAP BURNING COALS ON HIS HEAD." (Rom. 12:18–20)

The context of this passage is actually in reference to unbelievers which we have yet to discuss at length. That's why we can only extend peace as far as possible from our side. Believers who have the Holy Spirit, the Word, and their united identity in Christ, however, never have an excuse to not be at peace with each other.

Unfortunately, though, we can act as enemies when we sin against one another; issues may linger if fellow believers refuse to pursue peace. Or perhaps there are professing believers in the church who haven't actually been converted. In either case, we must continually draw upon the resources on our end to prevent resentment toward them, even if it's directed at us. When our gestures of goodwill are spurned, we can be tempted to react sinfully. Vengeance has many forms as already discussed: squeezing in a subtle dig, complaining to our spouses, or giving the cold shoulder. We may switch fellowship groups or services just to avoid our offenders. Setting them outside of our lives gives only a facade of peace. Even bottle-up anger is still a means by which we balance the scales of justice in our own minds. But Scripture commands us never to take revenge.

Paul implored the Roman church to leave offenses in God's hands, since He alone is just. No wrongdoing ever escapes His punishment. For unbelievers, God imposes His penalty with eternal hell. Would we really withhold peace from them and squander an opportunity to demonstrate God's love that may be used to bring offenders to repentance? For believers, as we just mentioned, God already poured out His wrath for offenders' sins on the cross. Do we really think more payment should be exacted because God didn't receive enough from Christ? The text reveals what our response should be instead of backbiting or cutting them out of our lives: serve them! We let God handle the offense; as a consequence, we are freed up to love our offenders by ministering to them.

Imagine a church where we're tripping over ourselves to be a blessing to those who refuse to be at peace with us, all while praying for their repentance. We bring them food and drink, spiritually speaking and perhaps literally as well, as we constantly find ways to do them good. We are actively *for* them rather than *against* them. Would this not make it challenging for them to remain in disunity?

As the passage states, God oftentimes uses this loving treatment to "heap burning coals on their heads" — that is, to bring people to repentance. Their consciences are triggered when treated as a friend while acting as a foe. God may use their contrition either unto salvation for unbelievers or a restored relationship for believers. Even if they refuse, Christ is still pleased by such behavior as exemplified in His own life on earth.

Strive for Evangelism

This last principle turns the corner to finally deal exclusively with unbelievers. While no less important, we cannot be effective peacemakers in our communities if we cannot first learn to maintain peace within the church. The two go hand in hand—our desire for peace with unbelievers flows out of our peace among the brethren. Evangelistic efforts cannot substitute or supplant our efforts to remain united in the body. Only when the church is at peace can we productively be proper ambassadors for Christ who plead with the world to take hold of the eternal peace He offers (2 Cor. 5:20). This is a critical act of obedience, since this is how God has chosen to save people. Imagine being granted peace with the Creator of the universe through no merit of our own and then selfishly refusing to share the message that imparts such reconciliation with our fellow neighbors. We must continually be seeking out opportunities to proclaim the free gift of salvation, "making the most of [our] time" to "make a defense to everyone who asks [us] to give an account for the hope that is in [us]" (Eph. 5:16; 1 Pet. 3:15).

The Reward

Future

Jesus used the future tense when promising the reward for peacemaking. He revealed that we "shall be called sons of God" (Matt. 5:9). Christ's use of the future tense most likely refers to His second coming. He will come and claim peacemakers as His children, not because we earned the title through our work, but because our behavior identifies us as those who have been granted salvation. We will be known by our fruit, just as "every good tree bears good fruit" (Matt. 7:17). He will claim us as children because He saved us; and our transformed hearts that pursue peace will serve as evidence. This adoption into God's family includes eternal life in heaven with Him and everything that entails. We will each be welcomed as one of His own.

Present

When we are faithful to practice peacemaking both with the church and the world, the latter recognizes we are different. We have the credibility of our transformed lives to stand on when sharing the gospel. Imagine what a community would conclude when they hear about the internal wrangling and arguing at a local church. They would dismiss us as hypocrites devoid of any power that can enact true heart change. Instead, we must labor in the Spirit to "appear as lights" among the "crooked and perverse generation" around us (Phil. 2:15). Moments after Jesus delivered the Beatitudes to the crowd by the Sea of Galilee, He remarked on the concept of God's children as light to the dying world: "You are the light of the world. . . . Let your light shine before men in such a way that they may see your good works, and glorify your Father who is in heaven" (Matt. 5:14; 16). Those whom God draws will perceive the stark contrast between this spiritual family overflowing with peace and their lives that have no peace or satisfaction to be found. God grants us the precious privilege of playing a role in His saving of others, but only to the extent that we are faithful to live out this supernatural peace. With that in mind, let's strive for peace that changes lives.

~

Blest are the men of peaceful life,
who quench the coals of growing strife;
they shall be called the heirs of bliss,
the sons of God, the God of peace.

~Isaac Watts, 1709

Questions for Reflection & Discussion

1. Reflect back on the past seven beatitudes studied thus far. How does the thread of humility run through each of them?

2. Why is the hope of "world peace" in our current state of affairs only wishful thinking?

3. Define *peacemaker*. Do you fit that description? Why or why not? Do you tend to seek out or avoid conflict? Why can both propensities lead to temptation to sin?

4. Imagine an unbeliever asks you what vertical peace with God is—how would you respond? Imagine an unbeliever asks you what horizontal peace with other believers is—how would you respond?

5. What is the peacemaking mission of the church to the world? What part are you playing in that mission?

6. Why is peace between believers always possible? Why don't they get along automatically? Why is it so important that believers maintain peace?

7. Review the list of conscience issues on pages 190–191. Which areas of personal liberty are you prone to judge others? With what biblical truth can you remind yourself to overcome this temptation?

8. Define biblical love. Do you intentionally exercise this kind of love? What three things can you do this month to practice?

9. Do you ever find yourself grumbling about a fellow church member or leader? What should be the right response? Why are believers "freed up" to forgive, love, and serve others even when they offend or have different views?

10. Is there anyone at your church whom you have not fully forgiven? Are there any signs of subtle revenge in your thoughts and actions that indicate this (such as avoiding him/her)? How can you serve him/her instead? Write down one act of service to render for him/her this month.

Chapter 9

Blessed Are the Persecuted

Blessed are those who have been persecuted for the sake of
righteousness, for theirs is the kingdom of heaven. Blessed
are you when people insult you and persecute you, and
falsely say all kinds of evil against you because of Me.
Rejoice and be glad, for your reward in heaven is great;
for in the same way they persecuted the prophets who
were before you.

John Chrysostom, a fourth-century church father, publicly condemned the lavish excesses of the culture's elite led by the Roman emperor's wife Eudoxia. Before his eventual banishment that culminated in his death, he preached:

> By the grace of God . . . I do not fear any present terrors. For what is terrible? Death? Nay, this is not terrible: for we speedily reach the unruffled haven. Or

spoliation of goods? "Naked came I out of my mother's womb, and naked shall I depart" (Job 1:21); or exile? "The earth is the Lord's and the fulness thereof" (Ps. 24:1); or false accusation? "Rejoice and be exceeding glad, when men shall say all manner of evil against you falsely, for great is your reward in Heaven" (Matt. 5:12). I saw the swords and I meditated on Heaven; I expected death, and I bethought me of the resurrection; I beheld the sufferings of this lower world, and I took account of the heavenly prizes; I observed the devices of the enemy, and I meditated on the heavenly crown.[1]

Kingdom citizens are commissioned to make the King known, not to refuse the privileges of suffering for Him. Moreover, this beatitude guarantees that *true kingdom living brings joyful suffering as we pour out our lives in service to our King who suffered for us.*

Our study of the Beatitudes has contained some unexpected twists and turns. The last one is no exception, providing one final jolt. Putting it all together, we learn that if we are poor in spirit, recognizing our spiritual bankruptcy before a holy God; if we mourn over our sin, grieving over its heinous nature and profound cost; if we are gentle, humbling our own wills underneath God's and living it out with the proper amount of force relationally; if we hunger and thirst for righteousness, desperately longing to know and imitate God's character; if we are merciful, desirous of and moved to alleviate the suffering of others; if we are pure in heart, partnering with God by the Spirit's power to pursue Christlikeness; if we are peacemakers, seeking to resolve all conflict within our church family as those who've been reconciled to God and extending it outward to the world; if we enter the kingdom and live within it as faithful kingdom citizens cul-

---

1. John Chrysostom, *Nicene and Post-Nicene Fathers of the Christian Church*, Phillip Schaff, ed., vol. 9 (New York: The Christian Literature Co., 1889), 253 (accessed online November 1, 2021, https://archive.org).

tivating these qualities and incurring the rich blessings He's promised for each, the final culminating outcome is persecution.

The message is clear: demonstrating the first seven beatitudes will surely precipitate the eighth. Imagine Jesus' disciples and the crowds reacting to this shocking capstone. While persecution isn't the reward, we can still cheerfully endure it as the means to the blessing. The joyful contentment that characterizes blessedness is possible even in a state of persecution. We must consider the inevitability of persecution, why it occurs, and the implications of it in our lives.

The Reality of Persecution

Living in a democratic free state, we are familiar with persecution being addressed in Scripture, but we tend to experience it as a lighter affliction. Perhaps we may not progress as far along in our careers, may be ostracized from certain social circles, or may even be increasingly pushed out of a place at the table of public conversation. These are not nothing, but joyfully enduring the disadvantages from our association with Christ seems feasible. But what if our children are murdered as a consequence of our profession? Or our families are uprooted and our homes destroyed? Or we are beaten and tortured? Such persecution is alive and thriving in many nations today; this is by no means limited to the Roman empire during which Jesus was preaching. These matters can quickly become much weightier, and yet the gracious, unmerited favor of blessing to persevere with cheerful hope still applies—even unto death. How is this possible?

Jesus' pronouncement of impending persecution is constructed in the past tense. The Greek verb implies an ongoing action perpetrated against them. The verse could more literally read: "Blessed are those who have continually allowed themselves to be persecuted." It's a continuous willingness to endure attacks as the price of godly living. Paul flatly warned Timothy, "Indeed, all who desire to live godly in Christ Jesus will be persecuted" (2 Tim. 3:12). Whether we realized it or not, the moment we became believers was the moment persecution began. This is overwhelmingly apparent in the Muslim world, for example, where a person is disowned or killed for converting to Christianity — either way, they are considered dead. But it's also true in every case since the enemy of our souls instantly commences his attacks when we repent and trust in Christ. As soon as we become new creatures, the devil comes for us, "prowl[ing] around like a roaring lion, seeking someone to devour" (1 Pet. 5:8).

The world and our sinful flesh are also waging war. While our culture still retains some limited connections to Christian ethics, it does not love Jesus; nor does it desire conformity to His image since "the whole world lies in the power of the evil one" (1 John 5:19). When the stark contrast between light and dark is exposed, the culture comes for us as well. The tempter also exploits our remaining flesh that "sets its desire against the Spirit" on its own (Gal. 5:17). As the intruder in our new hearts, our flesh continually kicks, screams, and chafes against our devotion to our King. War surrounds us and even rages within us.

With such enemies opposing us, we shouldn't be surprised at persecution. Peter reminded persecuted believers, "Do not be surprised at the fiery ordeal among you, which comes upon you for your testing, as though some strange thing were happening to you" (1 Pet. 4:12). Paul wrote to the infant church he had planted in Thessalonica not to "be disturbed by these afflictions" because, he reminded them, "you yourselves know that we have been destined for this" (1 Thess. 3:3). The Thessalonians had heard of Paul's difficulties in ministry after his departure, and they themselves were beginning to experience the first pangs of oppression. Persecution was ramping up for these believers who had heard and responded to the gospel most likely only a handful of months prior. But Paul had apparently already warned them that being targeted is the believer's destiny. He continued, "For indeed when we were with you, we kept telling you in advance that we were going to suffer affliction; and so it came to pass, as you know" (v. 4). Suffering was foreordained not just for the apostles but all believers.

Benjamin Franklin once penned, "In this world nothing can be said to be certain, except death and taxes."[2] We can confidently add Christian persecution to that list. We are going to suffer on account of our Savior. The attacks can run the gambit and manifest in different forms, but they have come, are coming, and will continue to come. It shouldn't surprise us, but many times it does! We don't understand why the world doesn't like us when we are intentionally loving them. It stings when extended family disinvites us to Thanksgiving because they're tired of hearing about Jesus. Rejection from those we care about is never easy. Just as painful are the rejections of the neighbor at the front door or the student on campus when they both scoff at our ignorance. Mocking our backward, judgmental narrow-mindedness, they despise the exclusivity of a gospel that confronts them as sinners on their way to hell. In those crushing moments, we must remember this is normal, predicted, promised, and expected.

The seventeenth-century Puritan Thomas Watson warned of persecution:

> The saints have no charter of exemption from trials. Though they be never so meek, merciful, pure in heart, their piety will not shield them from sufferings. . . . The way to heaven is by way of thorns and blood. . . . The children of God in their passage to the holy land must meet with fiery serpents and a red sea of persecution. . . . Set it down as a maxim, if you will follow Christ, you must see the swords and staves.[3]

2. Benjamin Franklin to Jean-Baptiste LeRoy, November 13, 1789, Benjamin Franklin Papers, Library of Congress, https://www.loc.gov/collections/benjamin-franklin-papers.
3. Thomas Watson, *Beatitudes: An Exposition of Matthew 5:1–12*, Christian Classics Ethereal Library, https://www.ccel.org/ccel/watson/beatitudes.html.

This has rung true throughout history. Believers have indeed experienced the swords, staves, gallows, guillotines, stakes, racks, and prisons. They've been drowned, maimed, raped, starved, and impaled. They've also been rejected, neglected, snubbed, mocked, threatened, hated, excluded, insulted, taunted, and scorned. If we faithfully proclaim Christ, we will experience some level of this. The darkness hates the light, so in this world persecution is the reality.

The Reason for Persecution

Impending persecution may be out of our control, but we must make sure that we're suffering for the right reason. We shouldn't suffer persecution because of our own foolishness or disobedience. Jesus was blessing those who suffer "for the sake of righteousness" (Matt. 5:10). Yet sometimes we feel we're being unfairly persecuted when the police ticket us for driving 20 mph over the speed limit on our way to church. That's not persecution—that's lawbreaking! Or perhaps we feel targeted when the IRS audits us for deceiving them on our taxes even though, we reason to ourselves, it's our money. In these instances, we are suffering for the wrong reasons. There's neither credit nor benefit to gain in those situations apart from redeeming them by responding rightly in repentance.

Peter summarized this concept:

> For this finds favor, if for the sake of conscience toward God a person bears up under sorrows when suffering unjustly. For what credit is there if, when you sin and are harshly treated, you endure it with patience? But if when you do what is right and suffer for it you patiently endure it, this finds favor with God. (1 Pet. 2:19–20)

The context in the passage was the height of oppression—harsh masters wickedly abusing their slaves, and yet Peter warned the believing slaves to ensure no sin on their part incited the malicious response. The apostle then offered up Christ as the paradigm for responding to unjust persecution, observing,

> For you have been called for this purpose, since Christ also suffered for you, leaving you an example for you to follow in His steps, who committed no sin, nor was any deceit found in His mouth; and while being reviled, He did not revile in return; while suffering, He uttered no threats, but kept entrusting Himself to Him who judges righteously. (vv. 21–23)

Our loyalty to Christ must always precede the demands of culture. After imploring would-be followers to deny themselves and take up their crosses, Christ declared, "For whoever is ashamed of Me and My words, the Son of Man will be ashamed of him when He comes in His glory, and the glory of the Father and of the holy angels" (Luke 9:26). When we are dedicated to serving Him, we will suffer. We cannot deny Him through behavior that fails to comport with the supernatural change wrought in our hearts. We must not compromise.

When I worked for a fast-food chain, a boss often instructed me to change expiration dates on food supplies in order to squeeze another day's use out of them. Cutting the corners allowed them to reduce waste and save money, but it was blatantly deceptive and against company policy. I had to respectfully refuse to do what my supervisor asked, knowing my noncompliance would appear trivial and cost money. I was definitely not popular for this stance, among many other matters, but that must be preferable to shaming my Master by allowing worldly pressures to dictate my decisions instead of Him. Many believers in the secular workplace no doubt deal with much weightier matters that may even cost them their jobs, but it's better to do right and suffer than to do wrong.

In other scenarios, we may obey God yet still err by being unnecessarily irritating when doing or saying the right thing. 1 Corinthians reminds us that love "does not act unbecomingly" (1 Cor. 13:5). Our righteousness should not come across as dishonoring, unseemly, improper, or rude. Otherwise, we may be rejected by unbelieving family or coworkers simply because our demeanor and delivery is needlessly abrasive or disrespectful. Instead, we must intentionally demonstrate an engaging and winsome humility that seeks to draw others in, not dares them to push us away. When the offense comes, let it be over God and His righteousness lived out through us.

The prophet Daniel exemplified this approach. He lived and worked in a pagan culture and yet never compromised his allegiance to God. For seventy years, he rendered service to a vicious empire that ravaged, captured, and enslaved his own people. In fact, his virtue earned him many enemies. As Darius the Mede came to power, Daniel was appointed to one of the most powerful positions in the government: "Daniel began distinguishing himself among the commissioners and satraps because he possessed an extraordinary spirit, and the king planned to appoint him over the entire kingdom" (Dan. 6:3). Naturally, his colleagues despised him for it and sought his downfall. They conspired to dig up some dirt on him and publicly expose him to the king, not unlike what happens today in our so-called "cancel culture," but their evil scheme hit a major snag. Pouring over the extensive records kept, they tried

> to find a ground of accusation against Daniel in regard to government affairs; but they could find no ground of accusation or evidence of corruption, inasmuch as he was faithful, and no negligence or corruption was to be found in him. (v. 4)

They couldn't find a single blemish on his record, which likely fueled their hatred even more, but the corrupt officials were undeterred. They decided, "We will not find any ground of accusation against this Daniel unless we find it against him with regard to the law of his God" (v. 5). They had to create a law just to be able to implicate him!

In Jesus' case, they just fabricated evidence, as "the chief priests and the whole Council kept trying to obtain false testimony against [Him], so that they might put Him to death" (Matt. 26:59). If we are going to suffer, let us join Daniel and Christ Himself by suffering for the sake of righteousness. Commentator William Hendriksen warned, "When the faith of God's children has developed sufficiently to be outwardly manifested so that those who do not share it with them begin to take notice, persecution results."[4] As we pursue faithful kingdom citizenship, cultivating the heart attitudes of the other beatitudes will usher in the last one:

> Those who faithfully live according to the first seven beatitudes are guaranteed at some point to experience the eighth. Those who live righteously will inevitably be persecuted for it. Godliness generates hostility and antagonism from the world. The crowning feature of the happy person is persecution! Kingdom people are rejected. Holy people are singularly blessed, but they pay a price for it.[5]

Fundamentally, persecution is inevitable for Christians because they reflect and represent their Lord who was Himself persecuted. Why should we as followers of Christ expect to receive better treatment by the world than He did? We should neither demand nor even

4. William Hendriksen, *Matthew*, vol. 9, *New Testament Commentary Series* (Baker, 1982), 279.
5. John MacArthur, *Matthew 1–7*, vol. 1, *The MacArthur New Testament Commentary* (Chicago: Moody Press, 1985), 220.

desire a warmer reception than our Savior. Jesus instructed His disciples:

> Remember the word that I said to you, "A slave is not greater than his master." If they persecuted Me, they will also persecute you; if they kept My word, they will keep yours also. But all these things they will do to you for My name's sake, because they do not know the One who sent Me. (John 15:20–21)

The world opposes those who live for Christ. Pursuing Christlikeness, which is the believer's mandate, will garner the same reaction that it did with Jesus and the church throughout history. Suffering and untimely death have never been distant companions. Though we may personally not live with these circumstances, there are many believers at this very moment who do. Simply being found with a Bible can result in torture and execution in North Korea and many Muslim countries in Africa and the Middle East. For these believers today, persecution is not theoretical.

Persecution has a long history; it came before the church was born, before our Master walked the earth, and even before Ishmael persecuted Isaac (Gal. 4:29). The roots of persecution date back to the very first family. Adam and Eve plunged humanity into a fallen world as a result of their sin. The account of their sons Cain and Abel demonstrates the reality of the curse as conflict quickly arose. Abel, a "keeper of flocks," brought God a sacrifice from the firstborn of his livestock (Gen. 4:2-4). Meanwhile, Cain, a "tiller of the ground," brought an offering from his produce (vv. 2–3). For reasons God does not disclose, He was pleased with Abel's but not with Cain's offering.

While God related in the Genesis account that Cain was infuriated to the point of murder, He revealed the inner workings of Cain's heart in 1 John: "Cain . . . was of the evil one and slew his brother. And for what reason did he slay him? Because his deeds were evil, and his brother's were righteous" (3:12). Cain was incensed with Abel's godliness: *I can't stand your righteous deeds because they make me look bad. They cripple my desire to think well of myself. I don't want to be around you because your obedience brings conviction to my evil heart. It assaults my selfishness, my self-sufficiency, and my self-pleasing ability to comfortably worship God any way I choose. Your righteousness drives me insane, and my hatred for you is growing every second that you and your moral superiority are still alive.* This is the attitude of sin, Satan, and society toward believers. It always has been and always will be. It's why John immediately followed that cautionary tale by reiterating, "Do not be surprised, brethren, if the world hates you" (1 John 3:13).

In fact, if believers are *not* being persecuted on some level, there may be a problem on *our* end. In an ironic reversal, true prophets of God throughout the Old Testament were persecuted by their own people who rejected His words. Instead, they welcomed false prophets who spoke whatever pleased their ears to hear. Applying the underlying principle to the self-righteous religious leaders of His day, Jesus chided them, "Woe to you when all men speak well of you, for their fathers used to treat the false prophets in the same way" (Luke 6:26). An ungodly society receiving our message well is cause for re-evaluation.

Sadly, a swath of mainstream Christianity today peddles a diluted gospel stripped of saving power and couched in appeals to satiate worldly desires. Like the false prophets, the world welcomes this message to take its place alongside the pantheon of other religions and humanist philosophies. There's a place at the cultural table so long as man's innate wickedness and inability to please God are never confronted, nor the exclusivity of salvation in Christ and the subsequent call to God-defined holiness insisted upon. The fact that some professing Christians in our culture are popular and praised does not indicate that the world is getting better and growing holier. It may simply mean that those invoking Christ's name are compromising God's standards of holiness.

The Specifics of Persecution

Insults

After mentioning the severity of physical persecution to the extent of martyrdom, insults may appear almost inconsequential by comparison. Surely enduring insults faithfully is easy. Sticks and stones are what inflicts pain, as the children's rhyme maintains — not words. But they do matter: Just consider our reluctance to knock on doors or stop strangers in the street to share the gospel. We're not in fear for our lives, but we do fear rejection, and many times that can manifest through a spectrum of insults. These unpleasant harangues may be rare, but the threat is real enough to dampen our evangelistic efforts. Whether they scoff, laugh, name-call, cringe, heckle, tease, yell, harass, sigh, curse, or just roll their eyes, their negative reactions to our message can fill us with a paralyzing dread. Sometimes we feel our ears burn with a mix of anger and embarrassment: *Here I am putting myself out there in my free time to do good for them, we reason, and they just throw it back in my face? I don't need this!*

We don't even need strangers to experience this; we can bear the brunt in the workplace, at home, or with extended family. Perhaps they flagrantly flaunt provocative, contentious speech in hopes of goading us into revealing that we're no different than they are. I had only worked for a week at another fast-food chain before an employee confronted me about my Christianity. "We're coming for you," he warned ominously. He promised that before long, they would make me look just like them. Verbal antagonism can definitely have a profound impact on our readiness "to make a defense to everyone who asks [us] to give an account for the hope that is in [us]" (1 Pet. 3:15). The stakes have only increased in our public climate which seeks to "suppress the truth in unrighteousness" (Rom. 1:18). They justify censorship by labeling our beliefs as intolerant, hateful, and even actual violence.[6]

---

6. Carl Trueman, *The Rise and Triumph of the Modern Self* (Wheaton: Crossway, 2020), 329.

Both in His life and in His death, our Savior was horribly insulted. During His ministry, He warned: "It is enough for the disciple that he become like his teacher, and the slave like his master. If they have called the head of the house Beelzebul, how much more will they malign the members of his household!" (Matt. 10:25) As Jesus demonstrated His great power and compassion for needy people both physically and spiritually, the religious leaders attributed His works to Satan! They accused the King of kings and Lord of lords who stooped to earth to sacrificially die as doing the bidding of the devil himself. This is the pinnacle of insult, tragically arising from His ethnic people whom he had chosen to preserve and care for throughout history. Christ's point was that His followers will be reviled and scorned for their identification with Him.

They repudiated His ministry up to the day He died. Even though He was shamefully stripped naked and viciously strung up on a cross, the verbal thrashings kept coming:

> And those passing by were hurling abuse at Him, wagging their heads and saying, "You who are going to destroy the temple and rebuild it in three days, save Yourself! If You are the Son of God, come down from the cross." In the same way the chief priests also, along with the scribes and elders, were mocking Him and saying, "He saved others; He cannot save Himself. He is the King of Israel; let Him now come down from the cross, and we will believe in Him. He trusts in God; let God rescue Him now, if He delights in Him; for He said, 'I am the Son of God.'" The robbers who had been crucified with Him were also insulting Him with the same words. (Matt. 27:39–44)

They literally added insult to injury, shaking their heads in derisive disapproval as their Creator was accomplishing salvation for mankind. The spotless Lamb was willingly surrendering His sinless life while the self-declared holiest men of Israel whipped Him with their tongue-lashings dripping with sarcasm. They thought Him cursed, not anointed. To them, He was the king of nothing. He failed to deliver them from the Roman empire, they concluded, and now Caesar's nails were justifiably driven into His hands and feet for claiming Sonship to God. Imagine gazing up at our bloodied, beaten, blameless Savior, soon to bear His Father's holy wrath for our wickedness, and dismissing Him as a foolish vagrant. Their promise to believe Him if He rescued Himself rang hollow, but it was His very act of remaining up there that confirmed Him as the true, long-awaited Messiah. The One who endured such verbal abuse warned His followers that we will share in His sufferings.

Physical Persecution

Clearly Christ braved more than insults. Sticks and stones accompanied those words to the point of death. He likewise foretold that His family would drink from the same bitter cup. In the middle of the Beatitude, Christ actually shifted from the third person to the second person, moving from the general audience to those who were actually kingdom citizens. In every other Beatitude, Christ spoke of "they," them," and "theirs." In verse 11, in the last part of the last Beatitude, when describing what kingdom citizens will undergo, He switched to "you" and "your."

It seems as though He was now directly addressing the primary group to whom He was preaching—His twelve disciples first and foremost, and then to believers in general. He made it very personal to the disciples as they gathered around Him on that Galilean mountainside. As the days led up to the cross, Jesus increasingly warned them that they would be harmed for His name's sake. History points to each of the apostles suffering physically for their faith, most to martyrdom, but the principle still applies to all kingdom citizens as well. For them and for us, Christ set the example of not reviling in return or uttering threats, but entrusting Himself to the Father (1 Pet. 2:21–23).

False Accusations

Christ also warned that His followers would bear the brunt of false allegations which also plagued the span of His ministry leading up to His death:

> Now the chief priests and the whole Council kept trying to obtain testimony against Jesus to put Him to death, and they were not finding any. For many were giving false testimony against Him, but their testimony was not consistent. Some stood up and began to give false testimony against Him, saying, "We heard Him say, 'I will destroy this temple made with hands, and in three days I will build another made without hands.'" Not even in this respect was their testimony consistent. (Mark 14:55–59)

Christians have been slandered, misrepresented, and scapegoated throughout history. In the early church they were accused of atheism, infanticide, incest, and cannibalism.[7] They were routinely blamed for various foreign and domestic troubles; the empire claimed the gods' wrath was incited for their refusal to worship.[8] They were accused of treachery for failing to recognize the divine status of the emperor, even though they sought to honor and obey the government to the extent their faith allowed.

Today, governments may label Christian sects as unpatriotic, rebellious, and dangerous. Many churches in China, for example, meet in secret as the communist government has cracked down on Christianity, viewing God's authority as subversive to the state's priorities.

---

7. Bart Wagemakers, "Incest, Infanticide, and Cannibalism: Anti-Christian Imputations in the Roman Empire," *Greece & Rome*, 57:2 (October 2010): 337–354, https://www.jstor.org/stable/40929483.
8. *Encyclopædia Britannica Online*, Christianity: "Relations between Christianity and the Roman government and the Hellenistic culture," accessed October 30, 2021, http://www.britannica.com.

Even in our own nation whose government recognizes free exercise of religion, true born-again believers are eyed by many with suspicion. Christians are increasingly maligned and pushed out of the arena of public discourse where legislation is codifying and mandating ideologies that fail to comport with reality. They redefine love, for example, so as to falsely accuse us of hate. How far persecution may develop here in our lifetimes is uncertain, but countries and kingdoms for centuries have already persecuted believers unto death.

The Reward of Persecution

What blessing can possibly come from persecution? Christ promised the "kingdom of heaven" and great reward within it to those who suffer for His name's sake (Matt. 5:10–11). Affliction, then, becomes an indication that we are truly citizens of God's kingdom. Persecution doesn't gain one entrance, but it provides a proof of actual citizenship, and thus becomes a source of joy. Peter observed:

> To the degree that you share the sufferings of Christ, keep on rejoicing, so that also at the revelation of His glory you may rejoice with exultation. If you are reviled for the name of Christ, you are blessed, because the Spirit of glory and of God rests on you. (1 Pet. 4:1–14)

Only believers experience persecution for the sake of righteousness because only we have Christ's righteousness imputed to us. Anyone else may suffer for the right or wrong he's done, but it can never be for the King's sake. Because they hate Christ, the world rejects those who seek conformity to Christ and desire the same for others. Jesus told Nicodemus, "The Light has come into the world, and men loved the darkness rather than the Light, for their deeds were evil" (John 3:19). He explained that "everyone who does evil hates the

Light, and does not come to the Light for fear that his deeds will be exposed" (v. 20).

Interestingly, the reward is the same as those who are poor in spirit. Not only do the first and last beatitudes share the same reward, but they also share the same present-tense verb: "For theirs *is* the kingdom of heaven." The other rewards are all pronounced in the future tense, looking ahead to His return when they will be fully realized. *This means that our spiritual transformation enables us to participate in the present aspect of the kingdom that God is building – the church, which He's growing and using to accomplish His work.* We rejoice that the kingdom is ours now since this is when persecution occurs, and the blessing is available. Once the King returns, there will be no more persecution which will also be a cause for great rejoicing. We will continue to partake of the blessings and benefits as He will usher in the future aspects of the kingdom in the millennium and the eternal state.

James declared as much: "Blessed is a man who perseveres under trial; for once he has been approved, he will receive the crown of life which the Lord has promised to those who love Him" (1:12). We are being blessed as we persevere, and we'll receive ultimate blessing when Christ comes again. This should motivate and encourage us to not give up or lose hope as we walk through trials. Christ remarked, "You will be hated by all because of My name, but the one who endures to the end, he will be saved" (Mark 13:13). We must recognize that persecution brings blessedness now and most fully in the future, "for momentary, light affliction is producing for us an eternal weight of glory far beyond all comparison" (2 Cor. 4:17).

Christ gave a further blessing in this compound beatitude that's structured in contrast to the others: "Rejoice and be glad, for your reward in heaven is great; for in the same way they persecuted the prophets who were before you" (Matt. 5:12). The command to be blessed is bound up in this reward. There's no joy to find in suffering unless it's for Christ's sake. The words in the original language for this imperative to rejoice are strong—we are to exult exceedingly, to continually jump

up and down in our hearts with an overflowing of joy. This is challenging to fathom, but the disciples were already faithfully obeying the
Lord's command soon after His ascension and the church's birth.

As the church was growing in Jerusalem, the high priest and
his Sadducean cohorts "were filled with jealousy" (Acts 5:17). They
viciously beat and imprisoned the disciples, but an angel broke them
out of jail, instructing them to teach in the temple. The temple guard
recaptured them, bringing them before the Jewish leaders who implored them to stop preaching Christ. Jesus had already prepared His
disciples during His ministry: "When they bring you before the syna-
gogues and the rulers and the authorities, do not worry about how or
what you are to speak in your defense, or what you are to say; for the
Holy Spirit will teach you in that very hour what you ought to say"
(Luke 12:12–13). Valiantly emboldened and supernaturally empowered, Peter spoke for the apostles amidst such rank persecution:

> We must obey God rather than men. The God of our
> fathers raised up Jesus, whom you had put to death
> by hanging Him on a cross. He is the one whom God
> exalted to His right hand as a Prince and a Savior,
> to grant repentance to Israel, and forgiveness of sins.
> And we are witnesses of these things; and so is the
> Holy Spirit, whom God has given to those who obey
> Him. (Acts 5:29–32)

The apostles courageously chose faithfulness to their Master in
the teeth of the terrors of persecution that enveloped them. Their holy,
reverential fear of God compelled them to obey their Savior's commission to go and make disciples (Matt. 28:19–20). Though they had
intended to kill them, the leaders instead had them brutally flogged
(Acts 5:33, 40). No doubt the searing lacerations on their bodies from
the whippings were still open, blistered, and stinging when they left
the Council, "*rejoicing that they had been considered worthy to suffer shame
for His name*" (v. 41, emphasis added).

This joy amidst the suffering pangs of persecution is available to each and every kingdom citizen. Believers can truly delight in persecution because it serves as assurance of the veracity of their faith. The same Peter, who went from buckling under the weight of servant-girls exposing him to boldly refusing to refrain preaching at the high priest's dictate (Matt. 26:69–72), wrote to others in a similar situation of persecution:

> In this you greatly rejoice, even though now for a little while, if necessary, you have been distressed by various trials, so that the proof of your faith, being more precious than gold which is perishable, even though tested by fire, may be found to result in praise and glory and honor at the revelation of Jesus Christ; and though you have not seen Him, you love Him, and though you do not see Him now, but believe in Him, you greatly rejoice with joy inexpressible and full of glory. (1 Pet. 1:6–8)

When Paul and Silas were beaten and imprisoned in Philippi, they were "praying and singing hymns of praise to God, and the prisoners were listening to them" (Acts 16:25). We are able to rejoice in suffering because we know it's for our Savior and for the purpose of making us look more like Him. In fact, God promises He will work "all things for good to those who love [Him] . . . to become conformed to the image of His Son" (Rom. 8:28–29). If our heart's desire is for comfort, peace, and as little resistance as possible from this world, we will never rejoice in tribulation. But if we long for Christ, our hearts resonate with Paul's desire to "know Him and the power of His resurrection and the fellowship of His sufferings, being conformed to His death" (Phil. 3:10). Our relationship deepens with our Savior through suffering in general, and persecution in particular. We do not exult in the pain itself—we grieve the affliction that causes harm, especially to those we love, but we praise God for the work He accomplishes through it.

He has already wrought His purposes long before us and the early church. Jesus pointed to the prophets before them who suffered "in the same way" (Matt. 5:12). The testimonies of these Old Testament saints should encourage us to remain steadfast. While some witnessed miraculous deliverances,

> others were tortured, not accepting their release, so that they might obtain a better resurrection; and others experienced mockings and scourgings, yes, also chains and imprisonment. They were stoned, they were sawn in two, they were tempted, they were put to death with the sword; they went about in sheepskins, in goatskins, being destitute, afflicted, ill-treated (men of whom the world was not worthy) wandering in deserts and mountains and caves and holes in the ground. (Heb. 11:35–38)

When we suffer, we are in good company with others who entrusted their lives to God by faith. As they anticipated their heavenly reward, so should we. Recounting this lifestyle, Paul observed,

> We are both hungry and thirsty, and are poorly clothed, and are roughly treated, and are homeless; and we toil, working with our own hands; when we are reviled, we bless; when we are persecuted, we endure; when we are slandered, we try to conciliate. (1 Cor. 4:11–13)

But he also reminded, "We are afflicted in every way, but not crushed; perplexed, but not despairing; persecuted, but not forsaken; struck down, but not destroyed" (2 Cor. 4:8–9).

Our mutual affliction as members of one body deepens our relationship that's united in Christ. We all identify with Christ through it, and others identify Him through us. Surprisingly, God uses our affliction to bring others to know Him. One might imagine persecution would have the opposite effect. Who would be enticed to adopt a faith that attracts such trouble to one's life? Yet God works through such powerful testimonies to draw others to Himself. Even in countries with authoritarian regimes, Christ promised to "build [His] church; and the gates of Hades will not overpower it" (Matt. 18:18).

Have we been compromising our faith or subtly refusing to pursue righteousness so as to avoid suffering? If we don't practice the first seven beatitudes, we won't reach the eighth. We will hope to skip over it, fearfully hedging our bets by dodging anything that might cause pain. We must repent of such behavior. By God's grace, I strive to share His good news with all unbelievers who cross my path, but I have also sat next to people and refused to share with them because I was ashamed. There is no excuse, though, because Jesus was not ashamed of us. He died for us so that we might do this for Him. Paul called on believers to remember what's true and be emboldened by it:

> Who will bring a charge against God's elect? . . . Who will separate us from the love of Christ? Will tribulation, or distress, or persecution, or famine, or nakedness, or peril, or sword? Just as it is written,
>
> "For Your sake we are being put to death all day long;
> We were considered as sheep to be slaughtered."
>
> But in all these things we overwhelmingly conquer through Him who loved us. For I am convinced that neither death, nor life, nor angels, nor principalities, nor things present, nor things to come, nor powers, nor height, nor depth, nor any other created thing, will be able to separate us from the love of God, which is in Christ Jesus our Lord. (Rom. 8:33, 35–39)

God uses believers' testimonies even beyond their time here on earth to continue the work of growing and preserving the church.

Just as Paul, the apostles, and the prophets before them left legacies of faithfulness to encourage us, so too did our fourth-century brother in Christ John Chrysostom. His encouragement through his writings has inspired many other fellow Christians to cheerfully suffer through persecution. We will conclude our study of the beatitudes with his reminder of Christ's promise that while we'll have tribulation in the world, we can take courage because He has overcome it (John 16:33):

> Walls are shattered by barbarians, but over the Church even demons do not prevail. . . . How many have assailed the Church, and yet the assailants have perished while the Church herself has soared beyond the sky? Such might hath the Church: when she is assailed she conquers: when snares are laid for her she prevails: when she is insulted her prosperity increases: she is wounded yet sinks not under her wounds; tossed by waves yet not submerged; vexed by storms yet suffers no shipwreck; she wrestles and is not worsted, fights but is not vanquished. Wherefore then did she suffer this war to be? That she might make more manifest the splendour of her triumph.[9]

~

Blest are the suff'rers who partake
of pain and shame for Jesus' sake;
their souls shall triumph in the Lord,
glory and joy are their reward.

~Isaac Watts, 1709

---

9. Chrysostom, Nicene, (1889).

Questions for Reflection & Discussion

1. What comes to your mind when you think of "persecution"? How often does it cross your mind?

2. Do you expect persecution for your faith? Why or why not? List at least two Scripture references that point to persecution for believers.

3. Have you ever experienced any form of persecution from unbelievers? If so, what? What was your response? Have there ever been times when you *should* have been persecuted but surrendered to the flow of the culture instead?

4. What should our attitude be regarding persecution?

5. Why can we never assume we will always live in a persecution-free culture?

6. Read Matthew 26–27 this week. Then read 1 Peter 2:21–23 again. What was Christ's response to persecution? How should this inform your behavior?

7. Do you regularly pray for the persecuted church today? Commit to pray at least once a week this month for those persecuted. What would be helpful things to pray for?

8. Do you have any fears regarding evangelism? If so, what specifically do you fear? What truths from Scripture can you apply to combat these fears?

9. How and why can we experience joy in the midst of persecution? List blessings that can come from persecution. Include at least two encouragements (specific verses) from Scripture.

10. How diligently are we pursuing the first seven beatitudes, knowing they usher in the eighth?

Conclusion

Who would imagine a book about blessings would conclude with the joy of persecution? Yet this is exactly where our Lord takes us in His sermon. How just like Jesus to continually overturn our expectations and tweak our sensibilities. We must not lose sight, however, of how we arrived at this conclusion. Persecution will be of no benefit or blessing to one who has not entered and pursued the kingdom in the power of the Holy Spirit according to the principles of God's Word. A thorough review and thoughtful evaluation are in order.

This begins with the very concept of blessedness itself. As we learned, to be blessed by God is to be the recipient of His unmerited favor and to find joyful contentment in His rich provision made for our salvation, sanctification, and ultimate glorification. True blessedness derives more from the life to come than our present condition. This stands in stark contrast to the world's desire to be "blessed" with the ability and opportunity to pursue their own desires and to receive the temporal comfort and stability this life may provide.

Next, personally reflect on each aspect of blessedness our Lord laid before us. Have you truly embraced a poverty of spirit? This recognition of our spiritual depravity will cause us to humbly admit that we have no ability in our inner man to provide anything of spiritual value for ourselves. This bankruptcy drives us to find our full provision in Christ alone.

Are you genuinely mourning and weeping over your sin, grieving over its deleterious effects and crying out to God for the grace of forgiveness? The rich fruit of godly sorrow will spur us to seek His strength in maintaining a willful determination to ruthlessly root out sin in our lives.

Are you growing in spiritual gentleness — the Holy Spirit-empowered ability to humbly and graciously exercise God's power in just the necessary amount to accomplish His purposes? We are never more Christlike than when exercising this grace which enables God's blessings to flow through us in tenderly caring for the needs of others.

Does the hunger and thirst for righteousness drive your spiritual appetite? Cultivating this craving enables us to recognize God's perfect standard, confess falling short of it, and pursue lives dominated by thinking and behaving in accordance with His holy character.

How is your mercy? When we are cognizant of and grateful for the mercy of God in our lives, we love to see others rescued from the suffering and affliction caused by sin. We will be willing to do the hard work of helping to alleviate, through biblical means, the affliction of those around us.

Are you deepening in purity of heart? Life in the kingdom demands growth in holiness as evidence of the reality of our changed hearts and renewed lives. The kingdom citizen has a single-minded devotion to God which leads to the passionate desire to be conformed to the image of Christ — the very reason for which God chose us for salvation "in Him before the foundation of the world" (Eph. 1:4).

And lastly, are you simply a lover of peace, or are you willing to exert maximum effort to bring reconciliation between opposing parties as a demonstration of the character and work of God? A life of active peacemaking enables us to confront the culture with its broken relationships toward God and others and to set a pattern for true harmony and joy.

A Final Exhortation

The twisting of our expectation for blessedness can be subtle. The enemy of our souls is crafty, and the wiles of our sinful flesh are cunning. It then behooves each of us to carefully and consistently study Scripture in order to have our thinking and motivations properly directed in blessed living. *This only comes through the spiritual discipline which the Holy Spirit Himself empowers.* 1 Timothy 4:7–8 reminds us that we must "discipline [ourselves] for the purpose of godliness," since it "holds promise for the present life and also for the life to come." Holy Spirit-empowered efforts in prayer, study, memorization, meditation on the Word, and fellowship with other believers in the local church are not outdated methods for legalistic fundamentalists, but the very lifeblood of spiritual blessedness.

Above all we must remember that Jesus truly is the King—the only One worthy of the total abandonment of everything in our lives except the pursuit of His kingdom. He is worth every ounce of the self-denial, suffering, and persecution kingdom living entails. My prayer is that the lasting outcome of reading this book will be the attitude of the apostle Paul who exclaimed:

> But whatever things were gain to me, those things I have counted as loss for the sake of Christ. More than that, I count all things to be loss in view of the surpassing value of knowing Christ Jesus my Lord, for whom I have suffered the loss of all things, and count them but rubbish that I may gain Christ. (Phil. 3:7–8)

If we lose everything and gain Christ, we have gained everything. This indeed is true blessedness.